GILPIN COUNTY PUBLIC LIBRARY

Wedding Styles

The radiance of three women helped the writer
steer between Scylla and Charybdis
Doris, my wife . . . Marta Hallett, my editor . . .
Edythea Selman, my agent.
J.V.S.

The Ultimate Bride's Companion

By Jules Schwerin
with Lily Laketon and Annette Spence

William Morrow and Company, Inc.
New York

A QUARTO BOOK

Library of Congress Catalog Card Number: 84-61404

ISBN: 0-688-02834-9

WEDDING STYLES was produced and prepared by
Quarto Marketing Ltd.
15 West 26th Street, New York, NY 10010

Designer: Liz Trovato
Editorial Assistant: Mary Forsell
U.K. Photo Editor: Sylvia Katz

Typeset by BPE Graphics, Inc.
Color separations by Hong Kong Scanner Craft Company Ltd.
Printed and bound in Hong Kong
by Leefung-Asco Printers Ltd.

First U.S. Edition
1 2 3 4 5 6 7 8 9 10

Picture Credits

KEY TO ILLUSTRATION CODES: tl: top left; tr: top right; bl: bottom left; br: bottom right; t: top; b: bottom; l: left; r: right; c: center

Courtesy After Six Formals and Alfred Angelo Bridals: p. 67(l). 70, 72(r), 87, 88(l), 89(l), 92(l)

Copyright © Alcindor Studio: p. 21(tr), 53(r), 68, 75

Courtesy Rosemary Arscott: p. 13(c)

Courtesy Artcarved Inc.: p. 31

Courtesy Laura Ashley: p. 18(bl), 19, 34, 46, 51(l), 98, 100–1, 101(r)

Copyright © Ginny Bissell, courtesy Anne Bransford Newhall: p. 54(t), 71(br)

Copyright © Camera Press Ltd.: p. 17, 83

Courtesy Bridal Couture: p. 53(l), 65, 89(tr)

Courtesy Bridallure, a Division of Alfred Angelo Bridals: p. 89(bl), 93(tr,br)

Copyright © Cecile Brunswick: p. 52(l), 71(tl), 73, 91(r)

Copyright © the Byron Collection, Museum of the City of New York: p. 16

Copyright © Colin Caket, ZEFA Picture Library Ltd.: p. 90(r)

Copyright © Jungkwan Chi, ZEFA Picture Library Ltd.: p. 82

Copyright © Lee Cushman Photography: p. 95(r)

Courtesy Jason D'Souza Designs: p. 45(b), 99

Copyright © Fabby, ZEFA Picture Library Ltd.: p. 29

Copyright © Michael Freeman, Bruce Coleman Ltd.: p. 26, 27(l), 63(l)

Copyright © H. Grathwohl, ZEFA Picture Library Ltd.: p. 91(tl)

Copyright © R. Halin, ZEFA Picture Library Ltd.: p. 36(l)

Courtesy Harrods: 45(t), 100(l)

Copyright © Gunter Heil, ZEFA Picture Library Ltd.: p. 21 (tl)

Copyright © Konrad Helbig, ZEFA Picture Library Ltd.: p. 27(r)

Copyright © Guido Hilderbrand, Camera Press Ltd. p. 57(l), 76–9

Copyright © Ken Howard, courtesy New American Catering: pp. 38–9

Copyright © Sam L. Jones, Photo Trends: pp. 42–3

Copyright © Tom Jones Photography: p. 12, 18(r), 20, 21(bl), 22, 28, 35, 37, 54(b), 66(tr), 71(tr), 72(l), 81, 84(l), 90(l), 94, 95(l), 96, 97, 104, 105

Copyright © Lynne Kanter: p. 58

Copyright © Dr. H. Kramarz, ZEFA Picture Library Ltd.: p. 103(b)

Copyright © Anne Lantzius, courtesy Anne Bransford Newhall: p. 60

Courtesy Lenox China, Inc.: p. 47

Copyright © Dana Levy: p. 41

Courtesy Lounette Bridal Veils, Inc.: p. 52(r), 61, 62, 63(r)

Copyright © Maison de Portrait: pp. 32–3

Courtesy Marionat Bridal Veils, Inc.: p. 64

Copyright © Marx, ZEFA Picture Library Ltd.: p. 36(r), 44(l,r), 85(l)

Courtesy Tina Michelle, a Division of Alfred Angelo Bridals: p. 30(l,r), 66(tl,bl,br), 67(r)

Copyright © Timothy O'Keefe, Bruce Coleman Ltd.: p. 23

Courtesy Piccione, a Division of Alfred Angelo Bridals: p. 86(l,r)

Copyright © The Piper Studio, courtesy Lorraine Rousseau: p. 69

Copyright © Prato, Bruce Coleman Ltd.: p. 91(bl)

Copyright © Tony Price, Adam & Eve Studios, courtesy Alexa Dedousis: pp. 48–9

Copyright © Gerard Schachmes, Camera Press Ltd.: p. 57(r)

Courtesy Jane Ranken Smith: p. 59

Copyright © Dr. Peter Thiele, ZEFA Picture Library Ltd.: p. 40

Courtesy Tessa Traeger: pp. 24–5, 80, 84(r), 85(r)

Courtesy Liz & Charlie Travoto: p. 13(l,r), 74

Copyright © The Whitman Studio: p. 55

Courtesy Andrea Wilkin: p. 50, 51(r), 88(r), 92(r), 93(l)

Copyright © Jonathan T. Wright, Bruce Coleman Ltd.: p. 102, 103(t)

Contents

Part One: The Weddings

By Jules Schwerin Page 11

Contents

Part Two: The Recordkeeper

Part Three: Our Wedding

Part Four: Appendix

Introduction

As we cross the threshhold of the computerized world of 1984 the super-romantic "white wedding" made famous by our great-grandmothers is returning to vogue—in its most expansive and traditional form. Although through the generations the wedding ceremony has experienced many transformations in form, there has been little dilution in its substance. Now we're seeing a rebirth of the convention of marriage in both traditional style and content.

The old-fashioned custom of getting married—with all its trimmings and trappings—has made a comeback. Although based on the traditional elements, the contemporary wedding conforms more to the style of the eighties. There is a reshifting of values and lifestyles, a return to fundamentals where the past is reexamined to fit the present and future. For the marrying kind—even for those doing it for the second or third time—there is the rediscovery of an agreeable institution—the wedding ceremony. The idea of celebrating, and honoring, a tradition as old as civilization itself is a refreshing change from the sixties, when couples were married before municipal clerks "downtown" or skipped the wedding altogether and went backpacking instead.

Today the bride doesn't necessarily wear white: She may be marrying for other than the first time. The wedding doesn't always take place at a religious site: The couple of the eighties may invest more spiritual attachment to the great outdoors. And the food served after the ceremony may not be the traditional roast beef or chicken dinner: Some couples prefer to serve their favorite foods, which may include sushi. All in all, based on the components of the traditional wedding, the creative couple of today runs the gamut from following a highly conservative tradition to a completely innovative breakaway from the standards.

The brides and grooms of today are different in many respects from those of a generation ago. The chances are that they are older and pursuing careers, each earning a living they will combine. Certainly they are better educated than their parents, and they may be better set financially than their parents were at the same ages. They seem to be a generation of people who are practical and realistic in their attitudes toward marriage, love, and sex. They know a lot more than their parents did of the same subjects. They know that the odds of achieving a perfect marriage may be realistically unreachable, but they are game to try it anyway, taking their chances for happiness with a partner with whom they may have already been living.

They seem to be inventing their own new traditions to fit the kind of marriage they believe in. When they are finally ready to put down roots and transform a relationship into a marriage, they are in search of a ceremony that respects their beliefs and their lifestyle, one that will evoke the spirit of their courtship, whether formal or not.

Though the counter-culture generation of twenty years ago alienated parents and children, today there is a predominant shift back toward family-oriented weddings. The traditional white wedding is definitely back in favor. With about five million people a year getting married in the United States alone, the move is toward getting married the way people did before the sixties, following the conventional traditions.

While the move tends toward the conservative style of doing things, the overall spirited freedom between men and women that grew from the sixties' rebelliousness has decidedly left its mark on the wording in the wedding ceremony for many couples. For instance, the phrase "Till death do us part" often becomes "For all the years that are to be. . . ." Many brides insist the word "obey" be removed from their vows. Many couples leave out the traditional Lohengrin *music with which to underscore the bride's appearance. Protestant and Jewish services, like the Catholic one, have accepted altered and simplified services to conform to the desires of brides and grooms and their families. And the bride and groom frequently blend traditional and popular music in the ceremony, and the churches and officiants cooperate.*

In most other respects, however, the form of the service remains intact. The groom and his best man stand before the altar and the officiating clergy while family and guests are seated in the pews. The groom's mood can be manly, resolute, or apprehensive. His bride, moving down the aisle on the arm of her father, brother, or male friend, is enveloped in white, dressed in silks or satins, perhaps stepping to the Mendelssohn theme. And the couple may be attended by bridesmaids, a maid of honor, a flower girl, and young pages. Whatever the scope of the traditional ceremony, and no matter how many people participate, the bridal party forms a striking tableau of regality.

It is customary to have a reception following the wedding. The size of the guest list, the time of day, and the budget for the event are all factors in the families' decision about the type of reception they want. The decision can range from a simplified at-home reception to a banquet in the church, a restaurant, hotel ballroom, or private club. A caterer may make things easier by supplying a photographer, florists, and music in a package deal. The wedding cake, the most important food accompaniment, is usually the focal point of the reception.

Here then is a survey of all the styles, both known and possible, for the contemporary wedding: the various styles ethnic groups use to celebrate the event; the various religious principles that shape the event for religious couples; weddings for every time of the year and time of day; and the range of possibilities and variations for each element. Each couple, hoping either to follow a prescribed style or create a new one for themselves, will find a full range of possibilities here.

Jules Schwerin

Part One:

The Weddings

By Jules Schwerin

The Announcement

A wedding is a public declaration of love between two people and has certain amenities attached to it.

First, the bride makes a guest list of all those who she wants to be present for the event, including her family members, friends, close acquaintances, and business associates. These are the witnesses who stand up for the bride and her groom. They make the event official. With the passage of the years, their presence in snapshots assembled in the wedding

The wedding becomes a reality for every interested party once the dated notice has been received—whether by invitation or announcement.

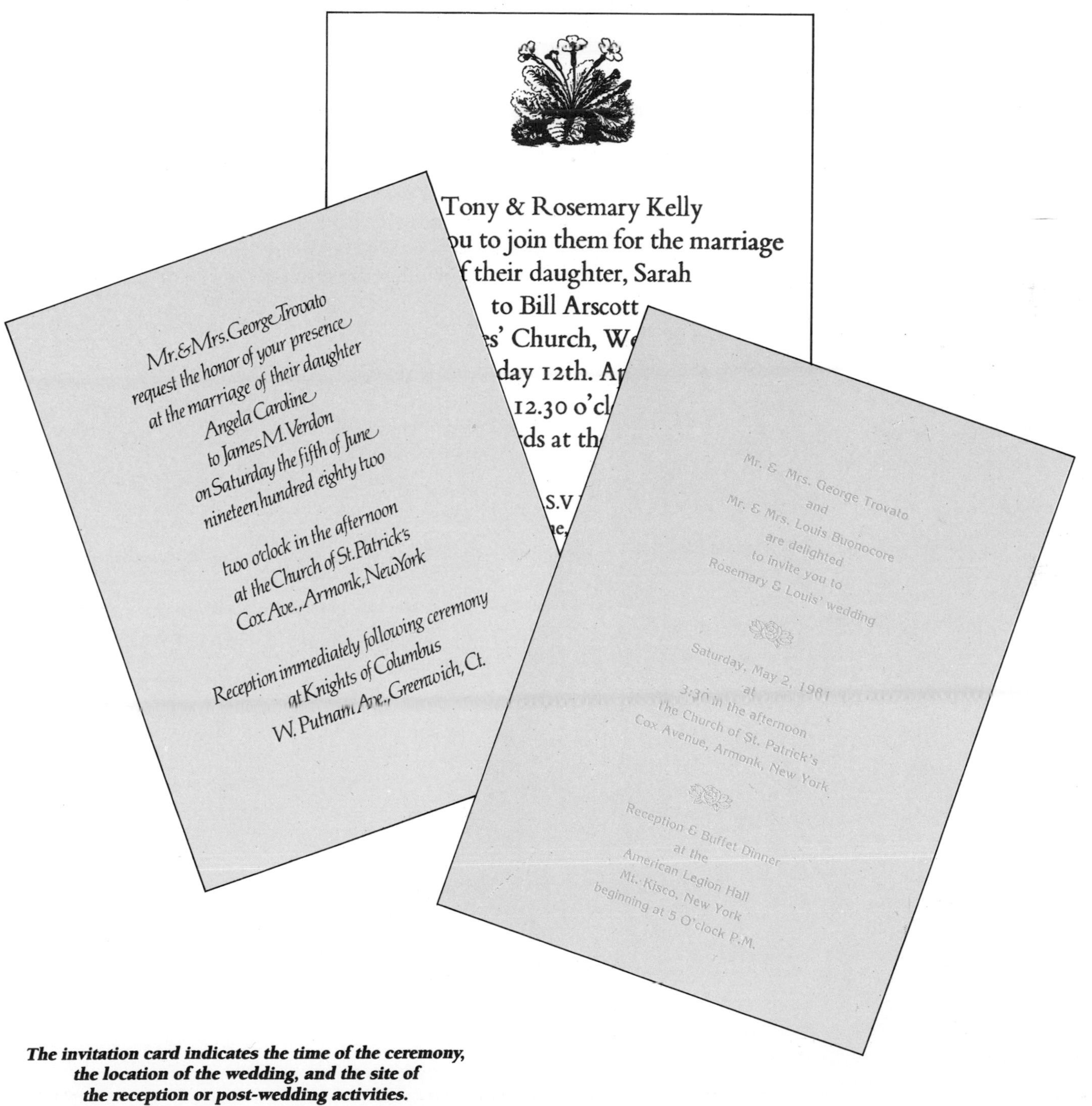

The invitation card indicates the time of the ceremony, the location of the wedding, and the site of the reception or post-wedding activities.

album gives the event the stamp of reality and permanence.

Second, the bride usually enlarges her list to include other people—friends and acquaintances of both families. To them, because they are not seen regularly, a wedding announcement is sent at a date that is close to or following the ceremony. Or, in lieu of the announcement, the wedding invitation is sent.

Usually the two families merge their guest lists, and someone is delegated to meet with the printer who will help in laying out and wording a suitable announcement and invitation card.

The announcement and/or invitation are usually mailed out to those on the guest list three or four weeks before the wedding ceremony to allow them time to respond.

A public notice is then mailed to local newspapers, providing essential information for the general public. These usually appear in the society pages and list the date of the event, the names of the bride and groom, and, customarily, the names of the more prominent members of the immediate families and their celebrated ancestors, if any.

No matter what level of formality the celebration takes, the public declaration of the union is an essential element.

WEDDING DAY
ITINERARY
11:00AM.
FAMILY BREAKFAST
THE BELLE-GRAE INN
515 W. FREDRICK ST.
2:00 P.M.
NUPTIAL MASS
ST. FRANCIS CHURCH
126 N. NEW ST.
IMMEDIATELY FOLLOWING
RECEPTION
THE BELLE-GRAE INN

Essential Information for the Invitation

The wedding invitation can be organized in a number of formats; however the following important information must be included:

- The fact that it's a wedding event
- Names of hosts
- Names of bride and groom
- Date (including year)
- Day of week
- Time
- Address of ceremony
- Address of reception
- R.S.V.P. request, with address

Keep in mind that "the honour of your presence" indicates a church wedding, while "the pleasure of your company" signifies a civil service.

Many families list every event for the entire day—the service, the reception, and some out-of-the-ordinary meals and events—to which every guest is invited.

Mr. and Mrs. William Taft McCall
request the honour of your presence
at the marriage of their daughter
Maureen Ruth
to
Mr. Theodore Stebbins, Jr.
on Sunday, the seventeenth of October
nineteen hundred and eighty-seven
at half after four o'clock
First Presbyterian Church of Encino
Sheridan Road and Balboa
Encino, California

Please respond on or before
October 7th, 1987

M ______________________

will ______ attend

Reception
immediately following ceremony
Dinos Lounge
4963 Balboa Avenue
Encino, California

Mr. and Mrs. William Taft McCall
announce the marriage
of their daughter
Maureen Ruth
to
Mr. Theodore Stebbins, Jr.
on Sunday, the seventeenth of October
nineteen hundred and eighty-seven
Encino, California

Miss Maureen Ruth McCall
acknowledges the receipt of your
Wedding Gift
and will take pleasure in writing
a personal note of appreciation
at an early date

Mrs. Theodore Stebbins, Jr.

The printer will usually suggest the style of invitation and announcement, one which will work with the character of the wedding. Here, the most formal type of invitation is shown.

A formal announcement is shown (above), with a standard gift card that will be sent to acknowledge receipt of the wedding presents by the couple.

The Victorian Wedding

A typical wedding portrait from the Victorian era shows a large wedding party, all dressed in the highest fashion of that time. Flowers played an important role in Victorian weddings, and an extended wedding party was very common.

Our great-grandmothers were romantic and sentimental women who nurtured the picturesque wedding ceremony that now has been revived not only in old photographs of family albums.

In an age that romanticized its own history, the Victorian wedding was generally a social embroidery greater than the wedding styles that came before and those of our own day. They set standards of excellence and high fashion we admire and emulate, but which, it seems, most of us can rarely afford in authentic versions today.

Victorian bridesmaids wore gowns made of white gauze on silk with deep collars often edged with fur. They flaunted wide folded sashes of colored satins. They wore hats of pale green or blue made of crumpled felt and often trimmed with colored plumes. The bridesmaids customarily passed through the guests at the service, giving out bouquets or sprays of white rosebuds mingled with white heather and lilies of the valley tied with a bit of ribbon.

Sartorial splendor was the name of the game for the gentlemen participating in and attending the Victorian wedding. They wore white carnations on gray morning suits with matching coat, trousers, and waistcoats, or the traditional black coats with striped trousers. Or sometimes frock coats with satin-faced collars and velvet ribbon trimmings were worn. Occasionally gentlemen wore silk-lined morning coats with pearl-gray ties and gray spats, black or gray top hats, and sometimes sported gold-headed canes.

The Victorian bride usually wore a conservative, white embossed, organza gown trimmed with velvet and a matching Juliet cap with a layered veil. The veil, which matched and coordinated with the ornamentation of the gown, was clamped over the forehead and usually fell to the gown's hem. She carried a spray or basket of mixed spring flowers, or she often cradled a bouquet of roses or lilies of the valley, orange blooms, and lilacs in the crook of her arm. Grooms placed the same flower in their boutonnieres that their brides carried in their bouquets.

It is a Victorian-inspired tradition for the bride to toss her bouquet into the crowd of her female guests at the end of the ceremony. The Victorian bride, however, usually held a few blooms as a memento of her very important day. Later she would dry the saved flowers and press them between the leaves of her favorite book.

A Victorian English clergyman characterized the symbolic meaning of the bride's bouquet this way: "It is typical of the gladness and dignity of wedlock, the crown on victory accorded to her for subduing the temptation to evil that had beset her on her virtuous course from childhood to matrimony!"

Brides often chose between plaiting their hair with a floral garland or wearing their long, unplaited hair as a natural veiling.

Victorian era wedding music was pretty much limited to "Here Comes the Bride" (from Richard Wagner's opera Lohengrin*—the Bridal Chorus) and "The Wedding March"*

Charming English pages play a unique role in a Victorian-styled ceremony, even today. Lace is typical adornment in Victorian weddings.

music (from Felix Mendelssohn's A Midsummer Night's Dream*—based upon the Shakespearean play.) Invariably these numbers were played on the organ that accompanied Victorian brides up the aisles of countless churches.*

Victorian manners in weddings were as stringent as they were in all social conduct of that time. Marital authorities were accustomed to expressing old wives' tales as though there were a rule of conduct or a general truth for the guidance of brides, and brides were susceptible to this advice. For instance:

Blue signifies truth, *white* purity, *and yellow* jealousy.

Victorian-style linens are a popular gift today for any bride and groom. The Laura Ashley linens shown here are always stylish and elegant—and utilitarian, too.

And so—

Married in white, you have chosen all right;
Married in gray, you will go far away;
Married in black, you will wish yourself back;
Married in red, you will wish yourself dead;
Married in green, ashamed to be seen;
Married in blue, he will always be true;
Married in pearl, you will live in a whirl;
Married in yellow, ashamed of your fellow;
Married in brown, you will live out of town;
Married in pink, your spirit will sink.

This contemporary new England bride* (left) *has patterned her gown, veil, and flowers after the Victorian style.

High-fashion is usually an adaptation of earlier styles. Here, a modern bride and her maid pose in the less formal, shorter length, afternoon wedding attire from London's Nick Ashley.

The Chap-Book

During the Victorian era many young women kept diaries of their dating years, noting down their "dates" as they occurred—both the memorable ones and those better left unremembered.

On the eve of her engagement to her "chosen one," the forthcoming bride would thumb through her cherished and well-hidden chap-book. Concealed from her family and friends alike, the chap-book was a cherished record of the men in her life—those already rejected or lost in memory—the gentlemen, as it were, of her acquaintance.

The chap-book contained blank pages on which the young women would describe the pertinent facts surrounding her meetings with young men. It was a time when young gentlemen were obliged to be introduced to young ladies, and young ladies, in turn, expected young gentlemen to be appropriately referenced and recommended. Applying all her creative talents to describing the day of their first meeting, she recalled what was eaten and drunk; whether a walk was taken or a trip in a new fangled automobile was the form of transportation; and personality traits, quirks of character, general descriptions of appearance, and, most important, whether she liked him or not. Frequently the young woman's comments would be diverting, uninhibited, amusing, or downright cruel—and there these personality sketches remain, nakedly revealed to the eyes of her descendants.

Although the Victorian-style chap-book is no longer used in the West, it is not at all uncommon for women to keep the chap-book form in personal diaries and letters to female confidantes. The exchange of letters between girl friends is especially appealing to those who prefer to share their romantic attachments with their peers.

Many fine novels and personal memoirs have been inspired by the diaries and preserved letters of young women who regard their youthful romances as worthy of remembering with affection.

The Flowers

In almost every instance, the choice of flowers and the floral arrangements at a wedding are guided by the season: the flowers which are most readily available and conform to the overall ambiance of the wedding. Formal weddings today tend to be bedecked with colorful elegance like the arrays provided by roses (pink, red, and white); delphiniums, which are the traditional blue flowers of bridal good luck; freesias (yellow, white, lavendar, and pink); lilies of the valley; and even carnations. Frequently mixed bouquets of spring flowers are used.

At the wedding site itself floral decorations can vary greatly, depending on the amount of money to be spent, the tastes of the bride and groom, and of course, the talents of the florist. One colorful method is to set bouquets on every second or fourth pew with an expansive display that integrates all the flowers in front of the altar. Some couples, how-

A champagne toast at the end of the service is a requisite salute to the newlyweds and is a joyous tribute to the couple's future married life together. Notice how flowers have been used here as decoration for the glasses.

In India, and the Eastern world in general, a floral headdress for both the bride and groom are customary. The flowers are local and were recently gathered.

This bride's long-stemmed bouquet lends a just-picked aura to her look, which makes her seem less formally attired.

The nosegay is probably the most popular type of wedding bouquet. Here, the bride has kept it simple by not mixing flowers.

Flowers can be used by the bride for decoration. Here, for the formal portrait, the bride and photographer display matching bouquets at the edges of her gown.

ever, prefer to limit the floral display to a smaller bouquet on the altar itself. Others combine flowers and tall candles along the aisles, although in this style care must be taken so that the flowers don't obscure the guests' views of the proceedings. If this is a problem, tall stands filled with flowers and ferns may be positioned behind the altar.

Besides acting as decoration, flowers are usually a part of the fashion accouterments for the bridal party. If flower girls are part of the bridal ensemble, for example, they may carry baskets of rose petals or other flowers' petals that they can scatter on the aisle ahead of the bride, or they may simply carry sprays or miniature baskets of flowers.

If the bride is not wearing white, then flowers in the same color as her gown or a complementary color may be used as decoration for the bridal party. Corsages are often given to the mothers, grandmothers, aunts, close friends of the couple, and sometimes even all the women attending the wedding. There is no rule against male guests wearing boutonnieres.

The groom and his male guests usually wear the same flower in their boutonnieres as the bride carries in her bouquet, and bridesmaids usually carry bouquets that complement the color of their gowns but differ from the floral combination of the bride's bouquet.

The theme of the flowers used in the ceremony is usually carried through and coordinated with the decorations used in the reception area, whether at the church or elsewhere. The head table and guests' tables will have centerpieces, and these ought to be simple enough and positioned low enough to be decorative yet permit guests to see one another and converse freely.

No matter how elaborate or how simple, flowers are an integral part of the wedding event. A subtle element that sets tone and style, flowers are part of the backdrop for the wedding environment and its participants.

At this outdoor Hawaiian wedding, both the men and women are adorned with flowers that blend beautifully with the surroundings.

Shapes and Combinations for Bridal Bouquets

Although lilies of the valley are favored as the traditional bride's flower, there are many other lovely possibilities for a bouquet. The simple elegance of a bouquet composed of white roses, calla lilies, and other mixes of long-stemmed flowers will make a gorgeous bouquet.

A cascading bouquet of gardenias combined with ivy and other shiny greens extending to waist level is a classically romantic combination.

Another charming possibility is the nosegay bouquet, sprinkled with a variety of delicate flowers. To make the shape of the bouquet more interesting, ask your florist to arrange the blooms in a crescent shape.

The bride can carry a basket of wild flowers on her arm, or make a more sophisticated statement with a single red rose. For religious ceremonies, a prayer book decorated with flowers can be a meaningful addition to the ceremony.

Decorate your bouquet in any manner that seems appropriate. A satin or velvet ribbon tied around the bouquet is an elegant enhancement. Above all, make sure the flowers you plan to use are available during the season.

Once known as the "groaning board," the wedding feast is the crowning glory of the wedding event. At this buffet-style table, the confections are as beautifully arranged as they are delicious. Besides pastries, candies are served. Notice how naturally the flowers play a role in the overall table decor. The glass and silver of the serving dishes combine to create a delicate yet classic display and elegant presentation.

The Hindu Wedding

India is a country where most marriages are arranged by the families of the bride and groom, sometimes even while the couples are small children. Few couples have any voice in the choice of their mate, or whether they wish to be married at all. Most often they are not even acquainted with each other, so the wedding acts as a bond between families, usually for social, political, or economic reasons.

While it is the essence of the centuries-old Hindu tradition to aim at a perfect union between husband and wife, honoring the bride as a future "mother of heroes," the couple may have such limited free choice and personal freedom in the matter that their adjustment may be frequently long and arduous, a relationship developing over a period of time.

At the wedding service, the groom ideally arrives in turban and veil riding a horse that is traditionally richly adorned with cloths and ornaments. He may come in a car or walk, should he lack the traditional accouterments. Either way, he is followed by a brass band that plays wedding songs. There may be dancers who are participating solely to entertain the onlooking crowd.

The service, which usually takes place in a temple or tent, begins by the couple taking seven steps together, symbolizing

The Hindu feast revitalizes the spirits of the guests with lamb, chicken, and vegetable curries; yogurt dishes; condiments (lemon pickles and chutney); mangoes; and tea. These traditional Indian foods are served in individual portions to each of the guests. It is clear from the number of dishes that this is a rather small, probably family-only celebration. The decorative designs of the dinnerware eliminate the need for other decoration on the serving table.

their journey through a long life. The groom recites a traditional mantra: "I am the word and you are the melody. I am the melody and you are the word." Then the bride places her foot on a stone, symbol of the eternal firmness of her devotion to her husband and the marriage. In turn, she recites other mantras. And finally the service is followed by the serving of refreshments and ritual herbs.

Later the bride will move into her husband's house, where his parents, not he, determine lifestyle. Traditionally the bride will make her way as a submissive newcomer in her husband's family. Only with the passage of time and strength of character will the bride and her husband carve a place for themselves with their children that is independent of the groom's family.

This newlywed Hindu couple is clad in decorative robes of bright colors that parallel the high festivity of the occasion.

It is not uncommon for a Hindu bride to take her vows when she is as young as eight or nine years of age.

Hope Cooke

When Hope Cooke, American society girl, traveled to Sikkim (a state in northeastern India with a population of less than 200,000 souls) in 1960, she intended to study Oriental languages. She lived with a wealthy uncle, an American diplomat, who had served in the Netherlands, Panama, Iran, and Peru.

Hope was having tea with some friends in the lobby of a Darjeeling hotel when she was introduced to her future husband, the Crown Prince, heir to the throne. His name was H. H. Maharaj—Prince Sikkim Palden Thoudup Namgyal. Shortly after the meeting he proposed to her and in 1963, on the death of his father, the Prince and Hope (renamed Princess Hopla, Consort of the Deities) ascended to the Sikkim throne.

Their wedding was a Buddhist ceremony, Hope having previously converted. They had over 15,000 guests who, in the course of the day and night festivity, consumed 400 chickens, 200 pigs, and 100 goats.

Hope wore a white silk dress, heavily ornamented with golden bracelets, and a heavy gold belt holding a scabbard with jeweled dagger. The king was dressed in yellow silk and gold brocades.

The Ring

Of all the wedding symbols that have survived through the ages, the ring is doubtless the most universal—always setting the seal of officialdom to the ceremony. Before the wedding the custom was and still is for a man to give the woman an engagement, or plighting, ring.

It all rests on the symbol that the circle itself represents: that it embodies magical powers. Historically the wedding ring has always been gold, with some allowance for exotic exceptions. (Gold was preferred, but plain gold is especially preferred because of the great value placed upon the metal itself, as well as the special character of the event.) Once considered a "holy contract," in which the groom guaranteed that he would love and cherish his wife forever, even providing for her should she ever be fated to be his widow, the ring expresses the joining of two people.

Traditionally a bride wore her wedding ring as part of a

The rings are perhaps the most enduring tokens of the wedding after the actual ceremony has taken place. Here the double-ring ceremony—where the bride and groom exchange rings—is shown.

Before a Kenyan (East African) tribal wedding, the bride's hands are painted with designs in henna, a reddish-black dye. Even her fingernails are painted for the occasion. Special experts are brought in to apply the paint, for it is a precise and difficult job, which requires artful application. The paint will remain on the bride's hands for one year, to exhibit her newlywed status among society. This painting has the same significance as the gift of a ring in a Western ceremony.

necklace that, as an amulet, provided protection against the evils of the world. While it is the custom for women today to wear rings on the fourth finger of their left hands, many Europeans wear their wedding rings on their right hands. Married ladies in the eighteenth century often wore their wedding rings on their left thumbs.

The idea that the ring in and of itself was magical may have evolved from a popular European belief that there is a particular nerve or vein in the fourth finger of the left hand that leads directly to the heart. Since the left hand is considered "the dreamer," the origin of the belief in a ring's magical characteristic becomes self-evident.

Though gold is usually the choice of material for wedding rings, there were times, prior to the nineteenth century, when silver was preferred to gold. Perhaps it was because more silver was mined and thus available at the time, or possibly because the price of silver rings was more attainable for the average person. In many European countries brides sported wedding rings with precious stones, while some wore rings on which the portraits of saints were painted or embossed. In Roman times wedding rings were set either with rubies or emeralds. The emerald was identified with the woman; the ruby with the man.

Betrothal rings today, as in the past, are inscribed with reverential inscriptions. A few that represent the lifetime commitment the ring signifies are:

"I am your friend unto the end."
"Be true to me, as I to thee."
"Your sight my delight."
"I do rejoice in thee my choice."
"To me till Death, as dear as Breath."
"My heart and I until I die."

A traditional accessory, usually used in a very formal wedding where there is a ring-bearer, is the ring-bearer's pillow, on which the ring is borne to the altar at the beginning of the ceremony.

Yet there were times and places, such as in puritan New England, where the practice of incorporating a ring in the marriage ceremony was actually discouraged by the church authorities. Rings, as material objects, were said to be "playthings of the devil," and congregations were reviled for their impiety when they strayed from the good path by exchanging and wearing them. More modern-day Quakers and Mormons discouraged the use of wedding rings because they were considered pagan artifacts.

When all the historical and traditional facts are considered, however, the ring seals a relationship that may endure forever. Shaped as a continuous circle, the ring has almost always unilaterally signified an endless love.

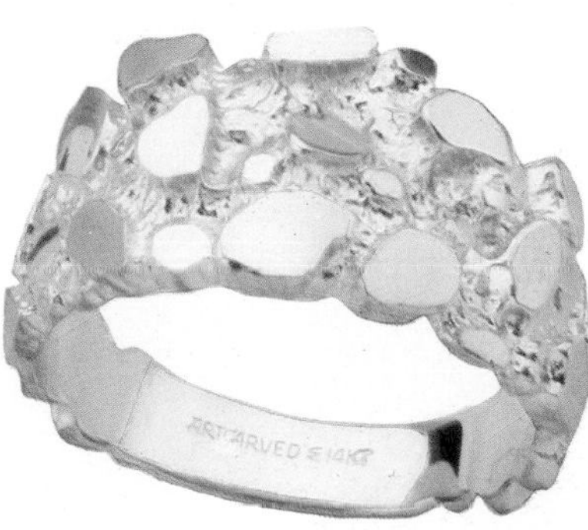

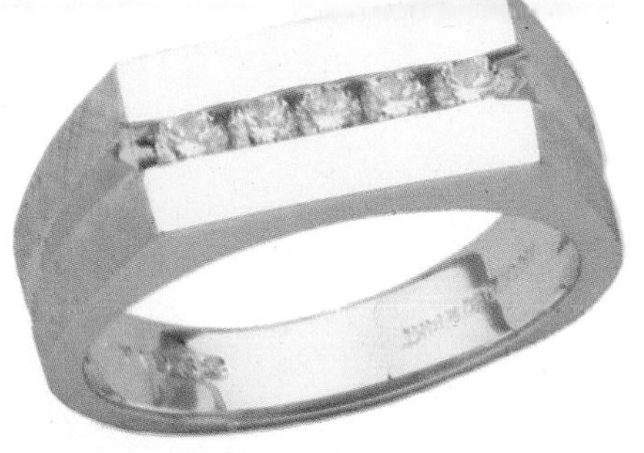

***Popular rings** (from top, clockwise): A handmade Florentine yellow or white gold band; a band with nugget design in yellow gold; twisted bands of yellow, white, and pink gold; a band set with three diamonds; a leaf pattern with three diamonds in two-tone or white gold; and a band set with five channel-set diamonds, highly polished on top, with Florentine sides, in yellow or white gold.*

The Cajun Wedding

A hundred miles or so west of New Orleans is Cajun country. There you'll find towns and cities with French-sounding names like Thibodaux, Houma, Jeanerette, Breaux Bridge, and Lafayette. It is a swampy land of graceful vistas, moss-dripping oaks, and people who speak a French patois of Norman and Breton seventeenth-century origins. A million people comprise this population of trappers, fishermen, cattlemen, and, with luck, owners of oil-rich land leased to the oil companies for handsome royalties.

Cajun weddings are traditionally Catholic. In some remote bayou settlements, the accordian frequently replaces the organ in a wedding service, where French is the preferred language. The most essential man in the parish is the priest—confessor and neighbor. Despite their strictness in following the faith, Cajun country people preserve a blind faith in sorcery, such as the credulous belief in loup-garous—

The wedding knot tied, a profusion of congratulatory toasts salute the bride and groom. The bridesmaid who pulls the ribbon that is attached to a ring will be the next to wed, according to Cajun tradition. Notice the elaborate cake and abundance of flowers.

Following tradition for a Cajun ceremony, here an unmarried older brother of the groom performs a solo broom dance.

werewolves—with a certainty that the devil roams throughout the countryside.

At the close of a wedding service, a bride's veil is usually covered with greenbacks pinned to it by her family and friends. When the cash contributions run out, she marches around the room proudly showing off her treasure, looking for all the world like a Christmas tree.

As the Cajun prides himself on his appetite for life, for being alive, he is consumed, if you will, with a love of good food, good drink, good dancing, and good love for one another. He'll tell you that any old excuse will do for all-night frolicking.

Weddings are especially happy times because of Cajun-style cooking, which is considered a high art. Crabs, crayfish, and chicken are eaten with the fingers. The table literally sways with the crushing weight of a Belshazzar's feast: fried chicken and rice; oysters and crayfish bisques; crayfish étoufée—braised crayfish in a Creole vegetable sauce—and gumbos of okra and rice, tomatoes, seasonings, shrimp, oysters, ham, sausage, red fish, shallots, and tomatoes. Every meal is an experience, and each one is punctuated by café noir, *an extra-strong black coffee.*

Should you be lucky enough to be invited to a Cajun wedding, and should you flatter a bride about her good looks and smashing personality, she'll be certain to look you straight in the eye, shrug her gorgeous shoulders, and roll her sparkling dark eyes heavenward. She might even try to answer you by saying something like, "You is tell me something what I is already know."

Traditional Cajun foods, expertly prepared, abound at the after-ceremony festivities.

Food And Feast

Some weddings begin the day with a festive pre-ceremony breakfast for the wedding party. Shown here is a sample setting for an elegant country breakfast that will precede a midday ceremony.

The wedding feast is de rigueur. *No wedding, simple or splendiferous, is official without one. The ceremony climaxes in the feast, and it has ever been thus. It serves many purposes: the social gathering of families and friends with the newlyweds as witnesses to the event; the reviving of flagging spirits of the guests and their hosts at the close of the service; and as a dazzling salute to fertility—the lush "groaning tables" of food and liquor, flowers, and music and dance—the siring of beautiful children.*

In the din of conversation, music and laughter, and the innumerable toasts to the bride and groom, one can trace the origins of this ubiquitous institution. The communal meal—the most important social ritual we practice—began when Eve handed Adam the apple. But a piece of fruit couldn't satisfy their insatiable appetites for variety. They foraged under the trees and in the swamps for the flesh of animals and vegetables to gratify their growing tastes, their yearning for more diversified foods. More than was necessary simply to keep them alive.

At the dawn of civilization, the communal meal of primitive peoples, sitting in a semicircle around a cave fire, turned them into social beings. (From those ancient times to our own, the custom of barbecuing meats over an open-air fire remains a pleasurable social event.)

When simple meals of single families evolved into tribal occasions—when grains and wild grasses became delectable additions to a meat diet—the repasts were splashier. Any excuse for celebrating their gratitude to the gods for keeping them alive through the winter, to experience once more the rebirth of spring, to share in the glory of abundant harvests,

Decorations like these local boughs and candles that are indigenous to a locale or season individualize a wedding.

Advantages of a Professional Caterer

Everyone has a friend who can cook, but hiring this person to cater your wedding could be a big mistake. A well-established, professional caterer may cost more, but you will have the assurance that everything will go as planned. A professional can actually improve upon your ideas and present attractive dishes that will harmonize with your wedding style. You can also feel confident that there will be enough food, that each guest will receive personal attention, and that the wines and sauces will be appropriate. Another attractive feature of the professional caterer is that your arrangement will be contractual and well defined, so the fee will be prearranged, and already worked into your budget.

the joy in the birth of a child, the arrival of the full moon, the return of herds of hunting animals, the death of a hero—all were acceptable reasons for feasting.

Nowadays, the banquet or the feast, if you will, becomes the occasion for all manner of rejoicing: from the most banal to the exalted—winning a lottery, the installation of a new officer of an organization, the winning of a sporting event or an Oscar. And yet the most esteemed celebration, the keenest desire of society to honor the life-force, is the wedding feast for the success of which nothing is too much trouble. It remains preeminently an excuse for surrendering to the pleasures of the table, whether at full-course dinners of roasts and fowl, fish and seafoods, vegetables and sauces, wedding cakes and fruit, nuts and after-dinner mints with wine, champagne, and mixed drinks, or buffets of hors d'oeuvres, cake, coffee, and drinks.

The glitter of the wedding table—glassware and plate, silver and place settings—carry over from the opulence of the Renaissance when the proliferation of the decorative arts made it possible for people of less than aristocratic rank to entertain in a kingly manner. In our own day, we try to maintain the traditions given birth then to what was known

In the East, as in the West, food maintains its symbolic meaning and thus is a crucial part of the festivities. Shown here, a wedding feast in India.

In Rumania the wedding party awaits their portions of grain at the reception. Grain, in its many forms, is a traditional symbolic element (of fertility) of weddings worldwide.

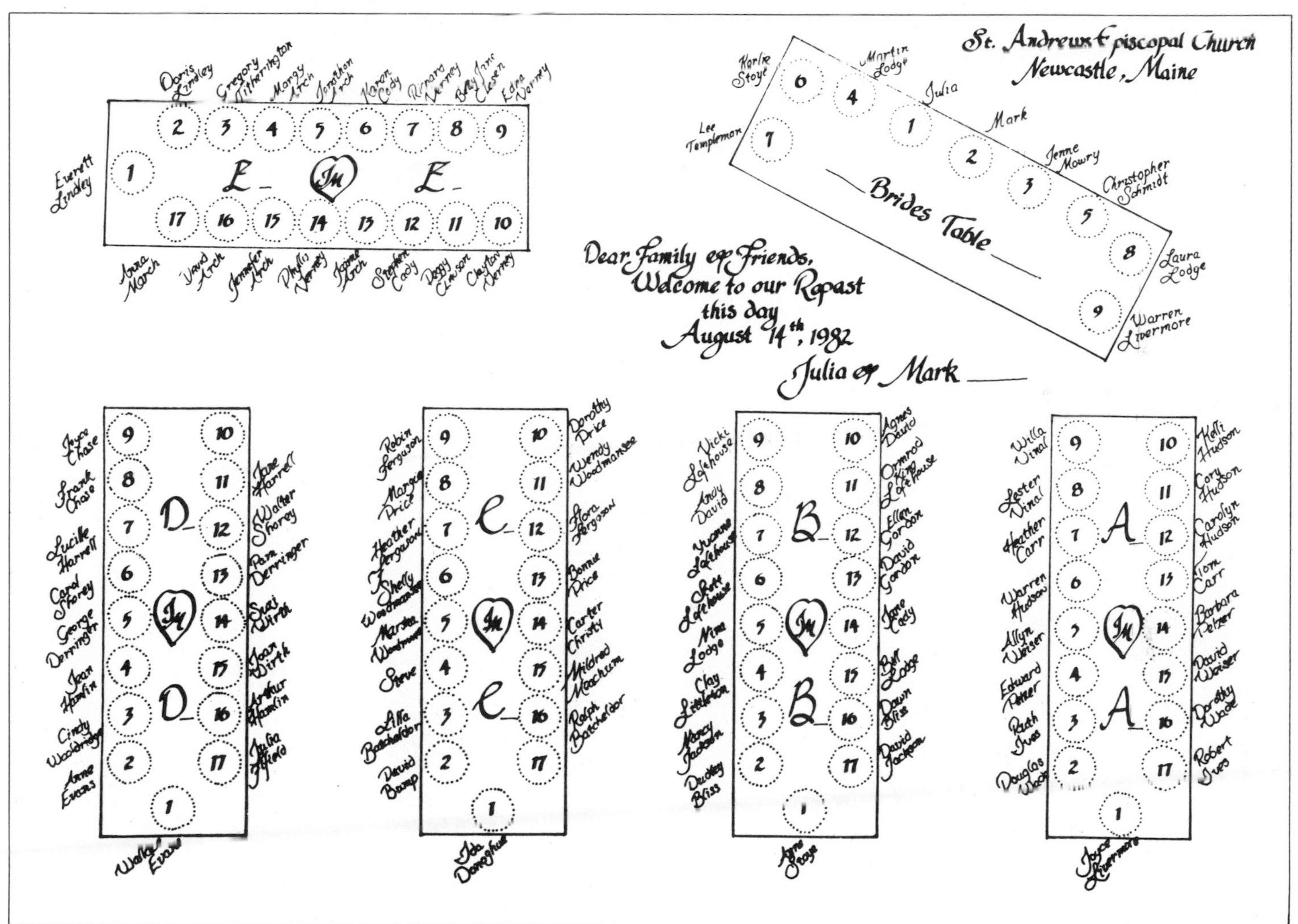

Rather than have the guests move from table to table to find their place cards, one innovative bride posted a beautiful seating chart at the doorway of the reception hall.

as "the polite society," the artful entertaining of the wedding feast. Aspiring hosts of such a creation can produce a memorable dinner party of good times with ease. The ingredients for the most brilliant of banquets are at hand in even the most pedestrian supermarkets, should catering the affair be unaffordable. However, it does require thoughtful, ingenious planning, and a respectable budget.

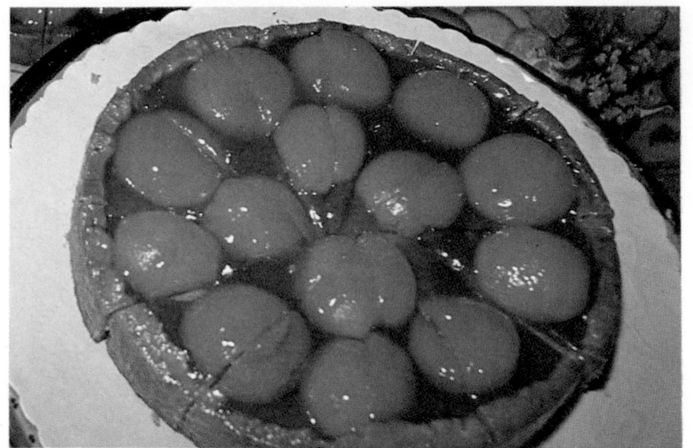

When a caterer plans her own wedding, goodies abound. Shown here are some of the sweets served at the reception, including a peach tart. Below, the all-important bread for the Jewish ceremony is displayed with sacramental napkin.

This fish-shaped mousse is covered with cucumber slices that are carefully placed to resemble delicate, translucent fish scales.

Crudités, a staple of less formal weddings today, are artfully displayed here with an ice sculpture.

The Japanese Wedding

The Japanese bride wears a floor-length kimono embroidered in silk or cotton. On her feet are white cotton* tabi *(mitten-socks).

Ritual plays an important role in the Japanese wedding ceremony, as it does in much of everyday Japanese life. Families of both the bride and groom share the cost of the wedding, which are usually held in small chapels or hotel ballrooms. In Japan, where there are three quarters of a million marriages a year, the families are estimated to pay more than $22,000 for a single ceremony. There is, decidedly, a traditional reserve and modesty attached to the wedding, although the younger set creates theatrical extravagances influenced by space movies and Western life-styles.

The so-called "arranged" marriage (omiai) *is still very popular in Japan and accounts for more than half of all the matches. In the past the arranged marriage was the duty of the couples' families; nowadays, a simple introduction, an exchange of photographs, or a well-orchestrated "blind date" is all that is required to choose a mate. The use of the computer in bringing singles together probably had its origin among the Japanese, and their families encourage the procedure.*

Usually the wedding is performed according to a simple Shinto ceremony. (Shinto is a state religion that teaches the existence of good and evil gods). This is followed by the couple's sharing a sip of ritual sake. The groom is often dressed formally in a cutaway coat, silk tie, and top hat; the bride is attired in a special, elaborate wedding kimono. Unlike her Western peers, the Japanese bride usually rents her kimono, and may even change dresses two or more times during the course of the wedding. These special wedding kimonos are particularly elaborate and may even be priceless antiques. The rental fee for the Japanese bride for her one or more wedding kimonos may exceed the price most Western brides pay for their wedding gowns, and they must be returned as well.

After consuming an elaborate banquet of Japanese delicacies and ice cream, the important people in the lives of the newlyweds are introduced—their parents, close friends, relatives, teachers, and employers. The guests, in turn, present gifts. Cash is especially appreciated as a gift by the parents, who use the money to defray the overall costs. Finally the wedding cake is cut and eaten.

Sometimes the modern Japanese bride will wear both a kimono and a Western-style gown during her ceremony. The change into Western clothes usually occurs at the close of the reception.

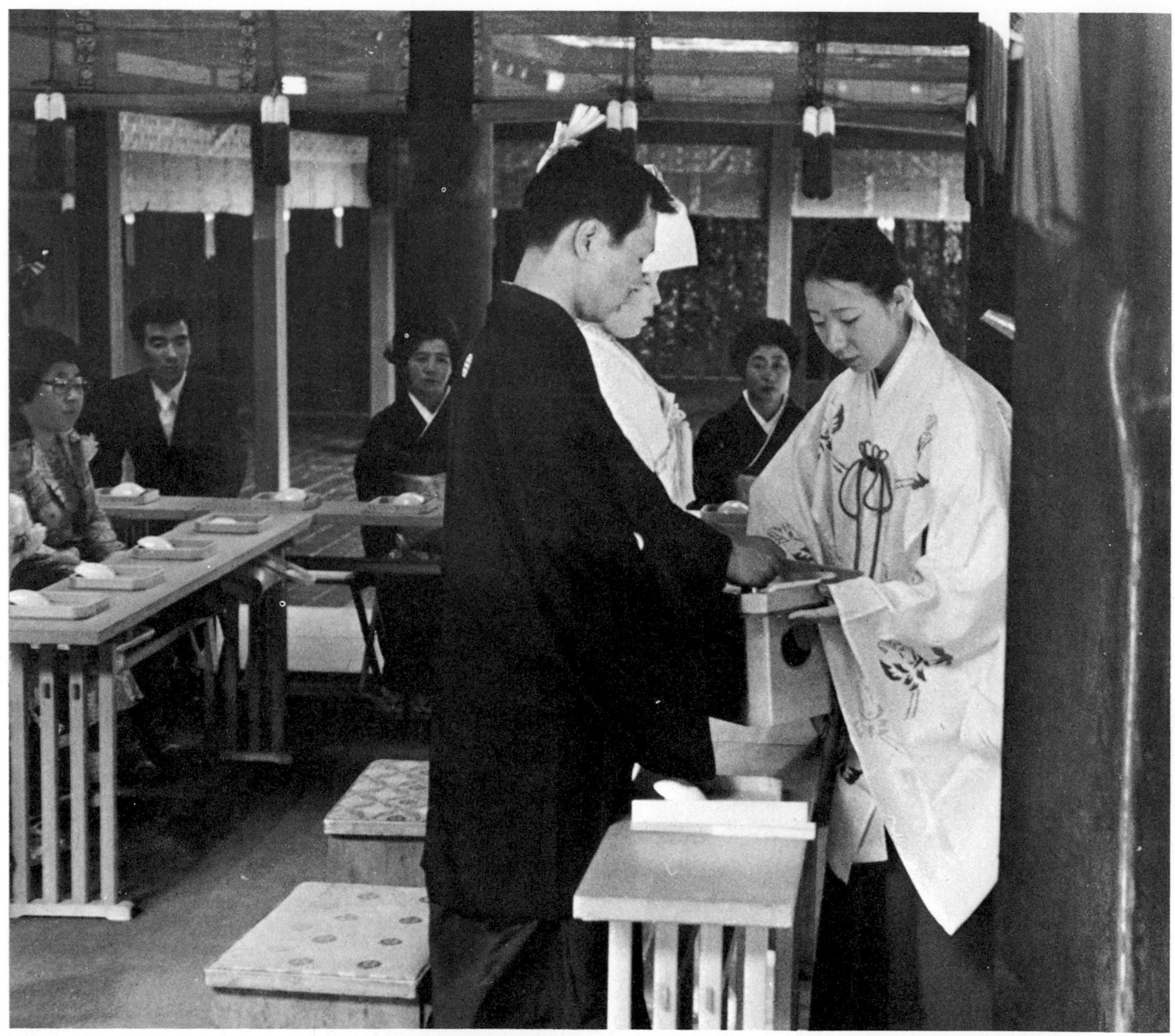

In the shelter of the Nogi Shrine (above), *a female attendant pours saki for the guests. Toward the end of the ceremony, the chief priest and his assistant conduct the* san san kudo *ritual, in which cups of sake* (right) *are poured and drunk by the bride and groom. The assembled guests also drink sake during the ceremony. At this particular ceremony, the bride touched her lips to the cup on numerous occasions, without actually drinking its contents. This marriage was arranged in the traditional Japanese way by the* baishakunin, *or go-between.*

The Gifts

In advance of the actual wedding, tradition has it that the bride's girl friends "shower" her with prewedding gifts at a cocktail party or a more sedate gathering where coffee and cake are served. The bride is honored by her circle of friends on the threshhold of becoming a married woman and leaving behind the golden heyday of her youth. From them she receives gifts considered useful in furnishing her future home: linens, dishes, kitchen utensils, stationery, books, or articles of clothing. Some showers have specific themes so that the bride receives gifts only for the kitchen or only linens.

The groom also expects to be feted by his male friends at a bachelor's party, traditionally a bit bacchanalian in spirit. It is the groom's last hurrah to his soon-to-be-lost bachelorhood, usually celebrated with good male friends.

In the days preceding the wedding, some brides choose to pay special honor to their bridesmaids by displaying the accumulating wedding gifts. This get-together is also used as an opportunity for the wedding party to be fitted for their ceremonial gowns.

Grooms often mark their engagement with gifts to their brides that are personal in nature: a ring of precious stones, a watch, or best of all, a treasured family heirloom like sterling silver inherited from a grandparent or a well-thumbed bible listing the births and deaths of the family members.

When Elizabeth I sat on the throne of England, it was the custom for the bride to receive at least one pair of scissors, which she was expected to cherish above all other gifts. The scissors were symbolic rather than utilitarian; the bride

In Eastern Europe the bride's dowry (left) is moved to her future husband's house before the ceremony. The future bride (right) assesses her dowry before it is actually moved.

Four Basic Prewedding Parties

1. The engagement party is the traditional setting for announcing your marriage plans. The couple or the bride's parents host the event.

2. The bridal shower is a gathering of female friends and relatives. Gifts are usually given in an afternoon tea setting.

3. The bridesmaids' luncheon and its masculine counterpart, the bachelor's party, are the occasions for the attendants to receive their gifts.

4. The rehearsal dinner traditionally takes place on the eve of the wedding. The couple may wish to invite only close friends and relatives, although for small weddings, all the guests can attend.

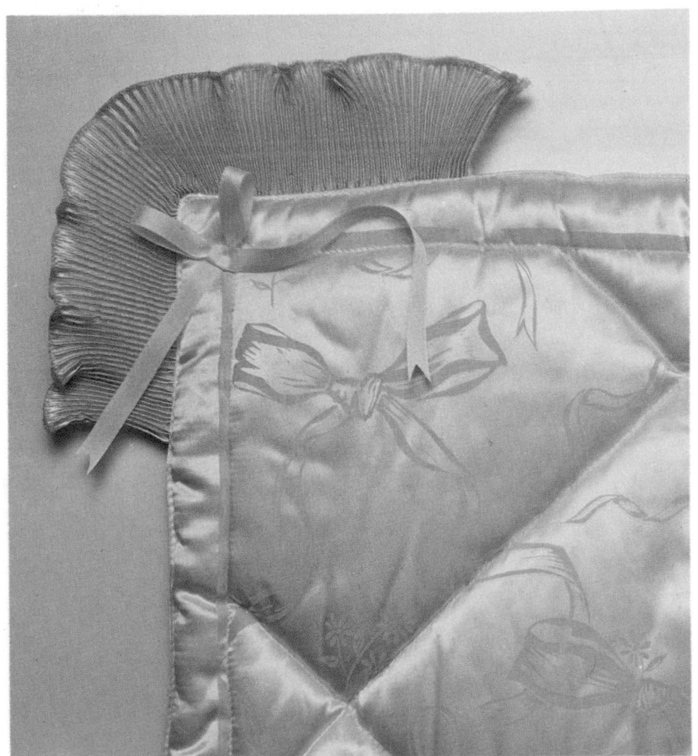

Stylish designs* (right) *in bedroom furnishings are always welcome wedding gifts, like comforters, sheets, and pillowcases.

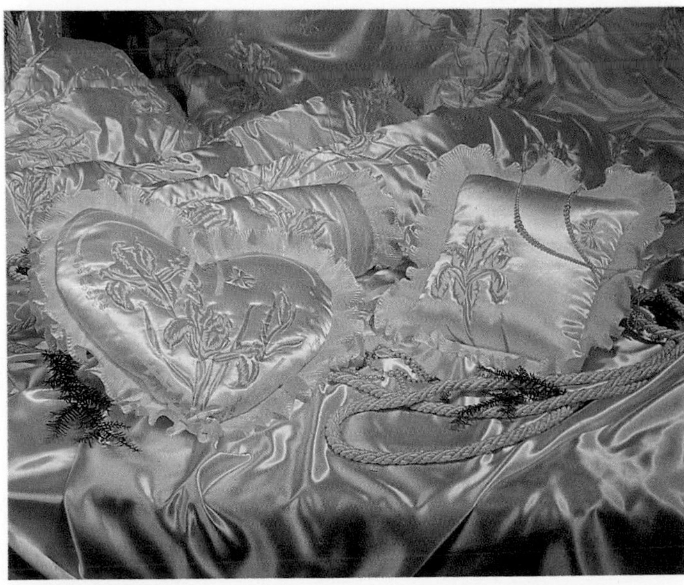

Embroidered linens, forever distinctive and personal make luxurious, elegant gifts.

could use them to cut the thread of happiness in the event that her husband should ever prove to be unfaithful!

From the most primitive society to the most modern, gift-giving to the bride and groom from family and friends is fundamental. As part of the accumulating dowry of the bride, the presents are proudly displayed: whether silver, stocks and bonds, cobalt-blue dishware from Rosenthal, a diamond watch, a basket of yams, or the plumes of birds of paradise. The fashion of gift-giving has its origins in tribal societies, where it acted as a yardstick for determining the wealth of the bridal couple embarking on a life together. Whether the wedding is modern and sophisticated or simple and casual, the accumulating wedding gifts are thought of as the bride's "earthly treasures."

Elegant country-home housewares for the future bride and groom are almost always good presents, as are these country linens.

A "breakfast-in-bed" set is not only chic, but is romantic, too.

The well-designed picnic basket here is a perfect accompaniment for the newlyweds' romantic outing.

China, in a pattern that has been chosen by the bride, is always a welcome and warmly appreciated gift.

Lead crystal, another traditional wedding gift, will set a table sparkling.

The Greek Wedding

The complex, colorful ritual weddings of the modern Greek Orthodox have undergone simplification over the years and seem to be modified by Greeks living out of Greece. Nonetheless, from classical times the sense of family and community has been very strong so that local cultural traditions are preserved to some extent no matter where weddings take place.

The wedding site—chapel, ballroom, or family residence—contains an altar with a copy of the Gospels on it. The room is fashioned with tall candles adorned with white satin ribbons, flowers, and plantings. The priest begins the service by making a sign of the cross on the bible while holding two rings. He touches the brows of the couple with the rings three times, then places them on their fingers. Prayers are spoken,

Dazzling chandeliers with lighted candles, floral designs on pews, and an impressive altar create a traditional Greek ceremony.

and garlands of flowers are placed on the heads of the bride and groom. The garlands, being tied together with ribbons, signify the union of the couple as one by marriage.

Also in the church, spoonfuls of a consecrated wine are taken by the couple and their best man. The ceremony ends with a prayer that is spoken by the priest honoring the couple's glory while they circle the altar three times, followed by the best man and bridesmaids, while their guests toss rose petals at them.

Even today, in Greek-American society, parental influence is very powerful in the choice of the marriage partner, the arrangements for the wedding service, and the serious details of the dowry. Though youths of Greek origin do meet casually in social situations outside of Greece, many of them retain a singular strictness in their initial behavior to one another. Once they become engaged, they and their families work energetically to build a solid financial base for the marriage. Moreover, it is traditionally important that the woman's honor be preserved before her wedding. Should she be suspected of having become dishonored, she can be severely punished by her father, or a brother may ritually take upon himself the responsibility for personally punishing her seducer.

After the wedding ceremony, the dowry is proudly displayed to the assembled guests. And then comes the time for feasting and folk dancing. The groom's father traditionally gives money to the musicians to begin the music. For his gesture he is honored by having the first dance with his new daughter-in-law.

Choosing the Time of Day

Depending on where you live or your religious per suasion, your preferred wedding time will vary.

For a traditional Catholic ceremony, you can schedule a very formal high mass at noon, a low mass at ten or eleven o'clock, or a simpler ceremony in the afternoon.

The Jewish ceremony is often held Saturdays after sundown or on Sunday afternoons.

Generally the Protestant ceremony takes place at noon or in the late afternoon.

Wedding time also varies by region. Midwesterners and easterners, for example, prefer afternoon weddings, while southerners tend to avoid the heat with evening ceremonies.

Today's elaborate marriage rites were founded in the beliefs of the earliest Christians. Here, a garland of flowers is placed on the groom's head.

The Bridesmaids

Thrice a bridesmaid, never a bride is an "old saw" repudiated by every bridesmaid with marriage for herself in mind.

At European weddings in earlier times, the custom was to surround the bride and groom at the altar with youths of their own age and acquaintances, dressed exactly like them-

"Vee," in wild silk, is electric-blue and pink with cerise net. "Andrea," made entirely of woven ribbon on organza, has a matching bag and headdress.

Andrea Wilkin's "Scarlet" is a short dress fashioned from silk duppion, a form of soft taffeta. The calf-length is most appropriate for an informal wedding.

Laura Ashley is famous for making the styles of the past work for the present. Here are three very casual yet stylized gowns for the bride and her maids.

selves so that any evil spirits lurking around could not pick out the marrying couple to do them any mystical harm.

That's why bridesmaids have been traditionally dressed alike and, until the nineteenth century, always in white. Nowadays, bridesmaids are dressed in a color that contrasts with that of the bride.

Bridesmaids frequently expect to receive a traditional gift from the groom. This is a carry over from the days when "marriage by capture" was the norm, when the bride's girl friends kept the groom away from her until he presented each of them with a present—in effect, a bribe to permit him to enter the bride's magic circle.

The bridesmaids' caps usually conform to the style set by the bride. This cap creates a less formal effect.

In a very formal wedding ceremony even the children in the wedding party are attired in high fashion.

Always an ornate touch to any wedding, whether formal or informal, a pair of flower girls precedes the bride.

These gowns display the ne plus ultra of elegant dress for the bride and her maids. All floor-length, thus formal, they range from those that are for day wear to those best worn for evening.

Duties of the Maid of Honor

The maid of honor helps the bride dress for the wedding and later for the honeymoon. She wears the groom's ring until the ring is called for during the ceremony. She assists the bride during the ceremony and signs the marriage license afterward as a legal witness. The maid of honor also organizes prewedding festivities, such as the bridal shower.

The ultimate in elegance at a formal afternoon ceremony: The bridal party is composed of the bride and groom, ten attending maids and groom's men, and the delightful flower girl.

Not only an accouterment to the ceremony, the bride's maids also usually help dress and relax the bride before the ceremony. The maid of honor is the last person to precede the bride up the aisle.

When great-grandmother was a bride, she may have sat for a portrait like this, surrounded by her attendants with their fashionable shepherd's crooks. Elaborate formal weddings such as this one are once again in style.

The Civil Ceremony

In New York City on February 29, 1984, the City Clerk's office of David N. Dinkins performed 138 marriages in the bureau's "chapel"—a small, windowless room containing a brass chandelier with stained glass panels on each side of the lectern. Each service lasted only somewhere in the vicinity of 45 seconds!

Typical of the couples who took the plunge that leap day, Pat Boonton, who works for a veterinarian, expressed the reaction of most of the civil service brides when she exclaimed, "Boy, that was fast." And her brand-new groom, James Sullivan, a florist, agreed, saying, "Yes, but it's for keeps," holding out the license for all the world to see. At the chapel in the municipal building, the marriage fee is still a modest five dollars!

The civil service is one that showed increased popularity during the seventies, but now seems to be receding in popularity. In North America it has been a popular alternative for a second union, and now, even in the Catholic countries of Europe, the civil service is fairly commonly followed. Naturally the more religious the cultural background of the couple, the more traditional the elements that will surface during the civil service ceremony.

Second-Time Marriages

In the United States alone almost three quarters of all weddings are second or third marriages for one or both of the persons involved. Three quarters of these women remarry within three years of their divorce. The "system" seems to have a most powerful attraction for even those whose "first time" was inauspicious.

Psychiatrists report that a second or third marriage is generally happier than the first and that it usually lasts longer. A maturing experience, perhaps resulting in greater forebearance in the relationship itself, contributes to the favorable odds for a fruitful second or third union.

The traditional white wedding with all the trappings is frequently replaced in second or third marriages by a less formal ceremony. The couple may simply prefer to go before a justice of the peace, to have a judge of their acquaintance marry them in a simple civil service in the family home, the judge's chambers, or at an informal brunch or lunch. Decorations in such cases are generally limited to the bride's floral bouquet or spray, and the couple may even propose that dress be informal. At such times, the guest list is limited to intimate family members and friends.

Second marriages often involve emotional and financial pressures that are different or similar to the first time around. Those who marry again often carry into the new relationship some of the baggage of a previous union: children, child support, and possibly guilt engendered by the previous marital failure. The fact of alimony adds an understandable stress to the second-time newlyweds.

Practically speaking, neither spouse in a second or third marriage has the legal obligation to provide support for his or her partner's children; nonetheless, the knowledge that such financial obligation exists and hangs heavily over the couple may unavoidably affect the mood of the new relationship.

It is a fact that a marriage unencumbered by children of a previous union will doubtless have smoother sailing than one that includes offspring of either partner. The presence of young children in the extended families of second or third marriages may, of course, actually be a joyful occasion, for these children as participants in the happy union can offer both moral support and expand the size of the wedding party!

In the United States, the civil service is commonly associated with leap year weddings. It is on this day that traditionally it is the woman's privilege to ask the man of her choice to marry her. Some men may even say, regretfully, that it's too bad that leap year occurs only once in every four years!

Even though the ceremony itself will be a simple affair, this bride embodies the height of informal fashion— and is accompanied by an equally fashionable groom.

At a French civil ceremony the bride and groom are elaborately dressed, and the official wears his magisterial uniform: A very private affair, this will become a special remembrance.

Veils and Headwear

Originally intended to conceal the bride from supernatural phenomena on the one hand and the groom chosen by parents in an arranged marriage on the other, the veil has become more transparent as it has become more symbolic. Today during the service the bride's face is usually visible through her veil. At the close of the service, it is customary for the bride to either toss the veil back over her head herself or have her bridesmaids help her pin it back.

Today veils vary in style and shape quite distinctly, and some of the most common types are crowns, wreaths, pearl-encrusted caps, pillbox hats, and even turbans. The length of the veil usually relates to the style of the bride's gown and indicates the level of formality of the wedding ceremony. A shorter veil is indicative that the ceremony is less formal, where a longer veil is worn for a more formal ceremony.

This bride's veil does not obscure her from view by the onlookers.

But brides alone are not the only ones to wear headpieces during the wedding ceremony. The bridesmaids very often have some sort of headpiece, usually flowers or a hat, and even the men in the wedding party may wear hats, which is almost always true for very formal ceremonies. Usually just an accouterment that evolved from bridal modesty in its earliest forms, today headpieces are either an element of stylish apparel or related to the religious significance of the event, thus following a sacred tradition.

During the 1940s when clothing materials were rationed, royal brides in England conformed to the rationing by using less material in bridal gowns and veils. Veils tended to be no more than shoulder length, and they were attached to a hat or a Juliet cap. Thus the attire of the bride was altogether changed specifically because of political and economic pressures.

After World War II, with the advent of nylon, the veil, which now incorporated the synthetics, took on a bouncy effect, and full-length gowns for both royalty and the masses returned to popularity. On occasion the single-tier veil gave way to two- or three-tier veils, the latter serving as a massive frame for the bride's face.

Varieties of Veils

Harmonize your veil with your complete wedding ensemble. For example, the long veil should extend at least a half yard beyond the bridal train, creating a very formal look. The three-quarter-length veil is accompanied by a short train. By contrast, the shoulder-length veil should be worn with a floor-length dress without a train. The silk illusion veil can be any length and is created by layering the material in circlets for a dramatic and romantic effect. Another variety, the blushing veil, is worn at Jewish ceremonies.

Probably only the hat in the foreground would suit a bride, but the others here would be delightful attendants' wear for an outdoor summer wedding. The attendants' straw hats connote an informal country look and would be particularly appropriate for attendants' dresses made of cotton.

Replacing the traditional veil, hats are still a chic alternative that also allow the guests to view the bride.

Photographer or Videotaping

There's hardly a married couple alive who doesn't cherish the collection of photographs of their wedding album filled with pictures of "those who were there with us." A few people have the special pleasure of being able to view the yellowing, crumbling stills of their parents' wedding celebration, and even their grandparents posing self-consciously in darkened photos.

Professional photographers who specialize in wedding pictures can be very good, or they can be awful. Their qualifications as photographers, their artistry and care in setting up the sittings, and informal coverage must be seriously considered.

Commercial photography for wedding pictures can, indeed, be expensive and time-consuming, and will cut into the couples' patience during the bustling time when the guests gather before the ceremony, and later, during the reception time.

One innovation to consider is the growing popularity of videotaping the ceremony. Most large cities have independent groups that service weddings with camera crew, lighting, and sound. It can be very professional and more expensive than traditional wedding photography, but worth it. A two- or three-hour edited tape is a sensational, dramatic commemoration of the event, one that can be screened again and again for the pleasure it brings the long-time marrieds and the new generation that wasn't there.

The length of the veil is determined by the level of formality of the wedding and by the formality of the bride's dress. Shown here are cap veils in the less formal shoulder-length **(left)** ***and the highly formal four-yard cathedral-length*** **(right).**

Here, the bride's headpiece is composed of a wreath and veil. The wreath can be made with either real or artificial flowers.

Although somewhat different from headgear in the West, this traditional headpiece adorns an elegant Indian bride.

These veils are the less formal shoulder-length, shown in both the cap and hat types. They are easily removed from the headpieces after the ceremony.

How to Toast with the Marriage Cup

A delightful European custom that will add charm to your reception is the ceremony of the marriage cups.

In France, the cup has a bowllike shape with two silver handles. Usually the cup is engraved with the names of the couple.

The Nuremburg cup is also silver and is a statuette of a young woman holding a cup atop her head.

After the couple vows commitment to each other, the bride then the groom drink from the cup.

Gloves And Garters

Some generations ago gloves were an essential part of dressing up. Until the last century brides were accustomed to receiving gifts of beautiful gloves from their grooms—gloves elegantly handmade of the softest leathers, sometimes bejeweled and embroidered. It was even the custom for the groom to present gloves to all of his important guests. Ironically, brides on the eve of their weddings frequently received gifts of gloves from some or all of their jilted suitors.

Gloves—whether white or cream-colored—though optional nowadays, may be "something old, something new." Obviously good taste in matching gloves to the bridal gown

Undergarments for the bride and her entourage should be chosen with care. Slips or camisoles should complement the dresses, and gloves and stockings should match. Shoes should be comfortable.

This bride has chosen a little something extra to add to her legwear, in addition to the "something blue" garter that she undoubtedly sports. These stockings hint at just a touch of elegance but do not overwhelm the rest of her outfit.

The shorter the sleeves of the gown, the longer the gloves can be. The length of the gloves is determined by the formality of the affair.

This lace glove with wide lace cuff comes in white and ivory. It is a perfect choice for the summer bride.

This bride has chosen to eliminate gloves altogether, whereas her maids wear elbow-length ones.

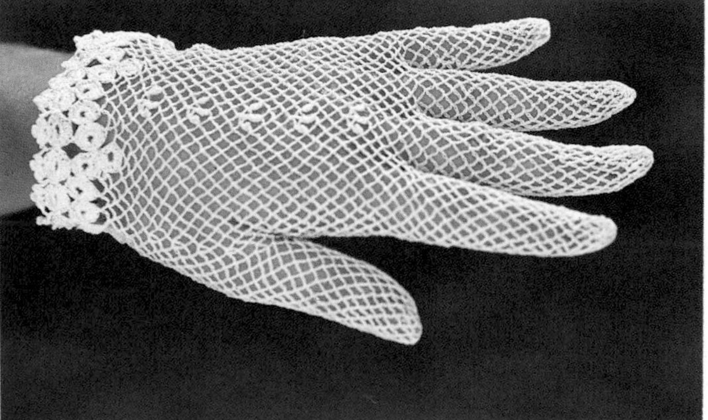

Crocheted gloves in white and assorted colors add the right touch to a formal summer wedding.

These fleurs de lis bridal pantyhose, in white, are for the bride who opts for a simple dress yet wants to make a striking impression.

This bride's gloves complement the lace on her gown and that on her veil, creating a subtle yet elegant uniformity of dress.

Some brides who choose outdoor weddings prefer a parasol as a head cover to that of a veil or a hat.

is a foremost consideration. If gloves are to be worn, then the bride must be able to remove them easily to receive the ring.

If gloves are "something old, or something new," then garters may be "something borrowed, or something blue." In the age of tights/stockings the garter is, strictly speaking, a bit old-fashioned, belonging to another time. Yet garters have always played a significant role in the wedding ceremony. They are still the most prized of the marriage trophies.

Modern-day guests have been known to scramble for the bride's garters, usually discarded during the reception. But there was a time when young male guests were expected to tackle the bride as she stood her ground before the altar. The successful brigand, the one who captured one or both garters from the bride, would loudly proclaim his victory while striding forcefully around inside the church. By tradition, and by prearrangement, the bride was expected to fall onto the floor, screaming. To put a stop to this at the wedding, it became the custom for the bride to distribute garters to her male guests "out of her bosom," so to speak. The significance of this ritual was that it reflected the bride's wish to lose her virginity through marriage.

At one time or another, grooms also wore ribboned garters on their legs, but history does not recall any incident in which brides or bridesmaids forcibly removed the grooms' garters during or after the wedding.

The color blue predominates in the history of weddings as being especially lucky for the wearer. "Something blue"—which may be old, new, or borrowed—is generally of a personal nature, such as a handkerchief, a hair ribbon, a piece of jewelry, or even the symbolic garter.

The Music

Without music, feasting, and toasting the bride and groom a wedding lacks dash and celebration. Regardless of the faith of the families, or their national origin, weddings are usually the time when traditional music is played, and social and folk dancing concludes the reception for the newlyweds. The music played before the ceremony, during the procession and recession, and for the reception will set the tone, mood, and atmosphere for the entire ceremony.

In the past poets were known to have composed special marriage songs for the occasion, while guests, bursting with food and drink, have customarily serenaded the bride and groom with popular songs of love. When families could afford lavish spreads, wedding festivities in Europe were carried on for a week or more, a sybaritic feverish time until the bride's family's money ran out.

For a hundred years, the bridal chorus from Wagner's Lohengrin *was the most popular piece of wedding music. Otherwise known as "Here Comes the Bride," this tune has, more recently, lost its monopoly as the accompaniment to the bride's procession. So, too, has "The Wedding March" from Mendelssohn's* A Midsummer Night's Dream. *Tastes have changed, and these two rusty members have been jostled aside, to be replaced by baroque music, fashionable canons like Pachelbel's, interludes from Handel's operas, a gospel like "When the Saints Go Marching In," or in the more extreme instances, by theme music from popular films like* Chariots of Fire *and* Star Wars.

It is still appropriate, however, for serious selections to be played during the service, while the more popular music is reserved for the reception. An increasingly popular trend, when "live" music is preferred, is toward chamber music rather than the more traditional organ renditions.

Once the service is concluded, the bridal party retires to sign the religious and civil documents. This is followed by the newlyweds' greeting of their guests. Toasts are poured (whether served to each guest or at an open bar) and congratulations extended. Then the ceremonial dinner follows, which may be served as a sit-down affair or as a buffet. And then there's more music.

This is usually the signal for the newlyweds to take to the dance floor. They are always given the honor of the first dance. They are then joined by other couples, who by now are usually in high spirits. At this point it is customary for the bride and groom to pair off with their respective opposite numbers in each family: the bride dancing with her father, the groom with his mother or sister.

An open-air wedding calls for an especially distinctive band, since the music must be heard above the sounds of the outdoors.

The type of music at the reception should reflect the personal tastes of the newlyweds. Here, folk music resounds with a classical touch.

The Groom's Men

The social psychologist will tell you that the best man role in a wedding has its origins in more primitive times when the groom decided to capture his bride-to-be and carry her off to his place, with or without her consent or that of her family.

It was the custom for the groom to choose a trustworthy friend as his best man whose mission was to distract the woman's family during her kidnapping.

Today the best man may be the groom's brother, best friend, or another relative. He is entrusted with the wedding

Before and after the ceremony, the best man is, traditionally, the groom's general factotum. He may manage the details of the wedding, but he is also conscious of not upstaging the groom.

Children are universally a wonderful addition to any wedding party. The ring bearer or page (left) is dressed to harmonize with these grownups in the wedding party.

The best man (right) oversees the groom's bow tie in that exquisite moment before the groom moves up the aisle.

The bride with his retinue—the groom and his men.

ring and traditionally stands behind the groom facing the clergyman. When the ring is called for, he is expected to hand it over to the groom.

As a general rule, the best man assists the groom in whatever chores may be required during the wedding rehearsal, working with the ushers and other guests with their attire and seating arrangements. He is expected to prompt the groom to bring the ring and the certificate of marriage to the ceremony. And he may, if required, assist the groom in dressing for the occasion and serve as a witness to the couple on signing their marriage contract. He may also be called upon to make the arrangements for a honeymoon trip, and be given the honor of offering a toast and reading congratulatory telegrams and letters during the reception.

The best man appropriately reflects the style and taste of the groom in his choice of wedding attire, whether formal or informal. Dark suit (navy, oxford gray, and black), tie to match, and black shoes. Or, more formally, a gray or black

The father of the bride is usually a member of the wedding party. Here, he is formally attired as he is about to escort his daughter into the church.

A bride and groom with their youthful attendants. The groom's elegant suiting is called "Silver Aston" and is the creation of After Six.

This sprawling lawn is an ideal setting for a wedding party outfitted from the vintage American South, with fans, walking sticks, parasol, and top hats.

cutaway coat with striped trousers, starched white shirt, a black and gray or white, striped four-in-hand tie, and black shoes and socks is customary. If the party is going to wear gloves, the best man and groom will wear gray gloves and black hat (most correct: gray or black homberg). Should the wedding be informal and the weather permit a garden setting, the best man might choose a white or cream-colored suit, white shoes and socks, and a light-colored tie.

The men in this wedding party are attired in a most tasteful and formal fashion: black cutaway coats, striped trousers, gray vests, wing collars, and gray ascots.

The Eighties Wedding

Some people used to be called "hip" in the years before the rise of the drug and rock music scene. For the past ten years, they're the netherworld of the "rockers," those who keep alive the disco fever.

Although they may, like the majority of the population, decide to legalize a personal relationship with a marriage, the service, if there is one, is reduced to the minimum, and is conducted, if at all, by a non-clergyman.

For an eighties wedding, appearance is almost everything. The couple usually sport ultra-high fashion. They may even display themselves in leather, levis, velvet, boots, chains, rings, necklaces, amulets, makeup, wing-tip collars, open-throated shirts or even bare feet. No matter what era they choose to represent at their wedding, this couple does it all with a flair for the most up-to-date fashions. Formal or informal, the attention to detail reinforces, once again, the rebirth in popularity of proclaiming mutual love publicly. But it's all done with a great deal of panache, and a little bit of devilish humor. Clothes will be trendy and unconstructed, and not necessarily what might, traditionally, be considered "wedding-style" attire. Music will be popular and nontraditional. Portraits and photographs will be informal and unposed, not regimented by standard settings and compositions.

Saturday
9:00 AM to 1:30 PM

9 AM 2 ZORBA THE GREEK
Zorba, caught in a fiscal crunch as the price of poultry soars, is forced to do his act with a rubber chicken. Zorba: Will Geer. Beppo: Charles Nelson Reilly. Frank Purdue: Himself.

4 CELEBRITY CHALLENGE OF THE SPECIES
Morris the Cat, Seattle Slew, Charo

9:30 7 THE EXERCISTS
Physical fitness for the possessed. Jack LaLanne, Ruth Carter Stapleton.

5 ARMENIAN GRAFITTI
Sir Kenneth Clark hosts a tour of the rest rooms and bus stations of this historic Soviet province.

10:30 9 LIZ AND CHARLIE'S WEDDING
George and Caroline Trovato (of the Armonk, N.Y. Trovato's) and Sidney and Dorothy Clough (of the East Aurora, N.Y., Clough's) present the wedding of their daughter Elizabeth to their son Charles. The wedding will be held at St. Patrick's Church, Armonk, N.Y. Live coverage of the reception, at 8 Byram Brook Place, begins immediately after. (See Close Up for details)

11AM 2 MAMMY AND THE PROFESSOR
The Professor has a surprise guest, old friend Rabbi Bronfman, and a big problem—Mammy is cooking hog jowls for dinner. LaWanda Page, Tony Roberts. Rabbi Bronfman: Jackie Vernon.

JULY 14, 1979

11:30 2 THE CLEAN PLATE CLUB
A mad nutritionist (Tony Randall) kidnaps neighborhood children and forces them to gorge themselves into coma. Big Mama: Angie Dickenson.

5 COHEN THE BARBARIAN
Marty Allen stars as a Semitic Soldier of fortune working freelance for Attila the Hun. Today Cohen wants to sack Rome right away because the local Athletic Club is restricted, but Wulf (Dick Gautier) reminds him that it's Yom Kippur. Attila: Burt Convy.

12:30 2 CHILDREN'S SPECIAL—"MOMMY WHAT'S THAT?"
Kippy (Mason Reese) takes a shower with Aunt Helen (Lois Nettleton) and is very confused. Mom: Anita Gilette.

1 PM 11 THE BARBARA WALTERS SPECIAL
Barbara interviews Al Fowler, a former key grip on Gilligan's Island, and Lorenzo Brancante, a protege of the late Louis Prima.

13 TALES OF TWO CITIES
Today: Waukegan, Illinois and Hackensack, New Jersey. Series host: Leonard Nimoy.

1:30 2 HOLLYWOOD GENETICIST
Wayne Rogers as brilliant Dr. Greg Mendel, the man who clones the stars. Today's episode: "Cher and Cher Alike."

close up

SPECIAL EVENT
10:30 9

LIZ & CHARLIE'S WEDDING!
Few social events since Tiny Tim's nuptials on the Tonight Show have aroused as much public interest as the wedding of Elizabeth ("Liz") Trovato to Charles ("Charlie") Clough. Howard Cosell will provide the blow-by-blow for the ceremony, scheduled to be held Saturday, July 14, at 10:30 A.M. at St. Patrick's Church, Armonk, New York. Rex Reed will cover the reception, at 8 Byram Brook Place, Armonk which begins immediately after. Among the scheduled highlights will be the cutting of the cake, endless toasts, interminable scenes of friends and relatives weeping unashamedly and four bridesmaids passing out on the lawn. (Program still being edited at press time.)

The bride and groom may get somewhat zany in announcing to friends and family their forthcoming wedding. Above, one couple had T-shirts printed with a logo. Right: Another couple patterns their announcement after the famous TV Guide format.

How the Married Name Affects You Legally and Socially

Whether to retain your name, adopt your husband's surname, or hyphenate the two is a personal decision. You will want to consider the practical legal and social aspects, although something so simple as how the names sound may affect your decision. Each choice comes with its own advantages and drawbacks. For instance, changing your name may trigger business and social complications; however it does simplify naming children. Keeping your name will bring you the opposite results but will recognize the issue of equality. Although hyphenating the names together would seem to eliminate all the problems, it could result in a complicated world of hyphenated offspring who will themselves want to marry someday.

If you do decide to make the change, you will have to amend a number of important documents, including your lease, voter and car registration, employment and investment records, Social Security card, bank and credit card accounts, insurance policies, driver's license, passport, and other vital forms of identification.

Here, simple elegance: The bride, groom, and bride's attendant pose daringly for an artful yet avant-garde photograph.

This eighties couple has chosen to hark back to an earlier era in styling their wedding outfits; yet they accomplish it so casually that they appear to be totally up-to-date.

The Computer and the Bride

In modern America, it's good to know that the biggest concern of the serious contributor to the bride's dowry—the duplicated gift—is now well on the way to oblivion. Although the bridal registry itself is not a new phenomenon, the advancement of efficiency by the new computer technology is a far cry from the original dowry, which the bride brought to her husband at marriage.

In advance of her wedding, most brides anticipate the arrival of gifts in duplication, or those which are the incorrect size, style, or do not conform to her sense of taste. The result in the past has been that a great deal of time has been wasted replacing and exchanging the duplicates.

But modern technology has come to the bride's rescue: major department stores are installing computers as their bridal registries. The procedure works as follows: the bride fills out a questionnaire with her preferences in silver, china, house furnishings, and other gift possibilities. This is done, often with her groom on hand, by scouting the department store or boutique for those items of personal preference. The form lists the size and color of the item, the pattern, and the manufacturer's name and identifying number. When the store has branches in multiple suburban communities, the computer provides out-of-town gift-givers with access to the bride's specific choices.

Each gift is registered on the computer by printouts as it is bought. This incredibly efficient method reduces the risk of duplicate purchases by gift-givers. Many stores will provide such information to gift-givers over the telephone.

Never conventional in the manner of tradition, yet following the barest guidelines of the ceremonial progression, the eighties wedding comfortably yet unconditionally commits the eighties couple to everlasting love.

This bride defies convention by wearing trousers, carrying a "bouquet," and wearing a headpiece that gives her accessories more emphasis than her basic apparel.

Because of the informal nature of their dress, the eighties couple can afford to lounge in their after-wedding wear without fear of wrinkles.

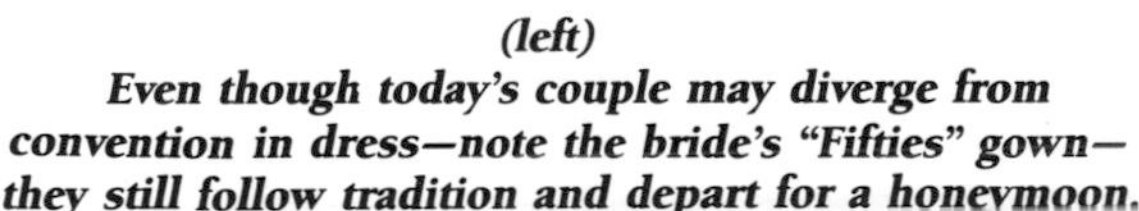

(left)
Even though today's couple may diverge from convention in dress—note the bride's "Fifties" gown—they still follow tradition and depart for a honeymoon.

This summer bride and groom are appropriately attired for the heat. She's wearing cami-knickers; he's wearing ever-stylish seersucker.

The Wedding Cake

No longer just an edible made with grain, solely representative as a symbol of fertility, the wedding cake has evolved into a primary decorative element for every stylish wedding.

Traditionally some kind of grain has been an essential ingredient of weddings as a symbol of fertility. Wheat, barley, and rice are the physical manifestations of this symbol. They participate in two ways during the wedding: throwing the rice after the reception and eating the wedding cake at the reception. Tossing rice into the path of the departing bride and groom as they leave the reception is one of the oldest wedding rituals.

Originally baked cakes made of wheat were the centerpiece of the post-wedding celebration, and to a great extent they still are. Additional ingredients baked into the cake have modified the original tradition with the passage of time. While the earliest cakes had a crumbly, dry consistency, bakers later became more artful and used eggs, butter, cream, sugar, spices, and pastes in baking their delectable labors of love. In Queen Elizabeth I's age, for example, spice and currant cakes were popular. Later small cakes were enlarged into a single bride's cake on which the given names of the bride and groom were elaborately decorated. At first these cakes were customarily broken over the bride's head; but eventually that custom came to be recognized as wasteful. Apparently someone decided that the cake was delicious enough to cut into small pieces and be sampled by the guests. And so evolved the modern wedding cake custom.

Wedding cakes are distinguished from ordinary cakes by the fact that they are generally constructed with two or more tiers. In addition to the traditionally iced congratulations to the bride and groom scripted on the top of the cake, various decorations—which may be alternatives to the miniature bride and groom—can attest to the interests and accomplishments of the pair: for example, a confection representing a musical instrument, sporting event, or the tools of a particular art or craft.

And some political and social figures have been known to prominently, and with pride, display the mouth-watering wedding cake, usually three tiers or higher, at the center of the feast table while celebrating the marriage of a family

This cake is considered less formal because it is composed of only two tiers.

This groom, twenty-five-year-old Toshimitau Kitanoumi (left), is a current grand champion of sumo wrestling. He and his bride survey the beautifully crafted wedding cake that befits a wrestler weighing four hundred pounds. The bride and groom are dressed in traditional Japanese wedding attire. In strictly traditional terms, it is common for the groom as well as the bride to wear kimono. The elaborate confection (right) was prepared for the second marriage of Dr. Christian Barnard. The unusual frosting cornucopia on top is, in itself, a major architectural feat.

The traditional cutting of the cake is one of the first joint ventures of the newlyweds.

Sequence of Wedding Reception Events

The purpose of the wedding reception is to greet the newlyweds, celebrate their marriage, and see them off on their first journey together as husband and wife. Traditionally the reception follows a sequence of events. First, the wedding party and the couple's parents form a receiving line. The guests then sign the guest book. Afterward there is the toasting, the cutting and eating of the cake, and the dancing. Amid or after the dancing, the bride tosses the bouquet among her female guests, followed by the popular garter throwing ceremony. Finally the newly married couple leaves the reception with rice and confetti strewn in their path.

This simple yet beautiful cake is styled perfectly for an informal wedding that maintains a conventional structure and format without excessive frills.

At this Rumanian wedding feast, (left) *grain is served in lieu of a cake. The grain, as a symbol of fertility, is representative of the ever-present traditions still in use.*

member. A wedding ring, for example, was baked into the wedding cake of President Wilson's second daughter, Jessie. Lyndon Johnson's daughter, Luci, was presented with a six-tiered cake consisting of sugar icing lilies of the valley and graceful arches. And Tricia Nixon, married in the White House, made the ceremonial first cut into an oversized lemon sponge cake that had been made with dozens of egg whites; later when the White House publicity staff released the list of ingredients to the press, there was an immense outcry from citizens who could not afford to duplicate the White House creation. The White House baker was obliged to simplify the quantity and cost of the ingredients of the cake for the ordinary customer.

Today it is traditional for unmarried female guests to receive a piece of cake to place under their pillows, supposedly enhancing their luck in finding a lifetime mate and a dream of their future husbands. To dream is, naturally, to make it so.

If the wedding reception features a buffet, the cake will probably rest on a separate table, to be cut after the toasts and before the meal.

The Bride And Groom

What is appropriate for the occasion depends on whether the wedding is formal or informal. Obviously good taste in choice of style and color is a major consideration for those with the responsibility of planning a wedding. Thought must be given to the overall cost of the affair, which traditionally is expected to be borne in large part by the bride's family.

One is accustomed to remarking that all brides are beautiful. And so they are, each in her own way. Yet beauty is

This bride showcases her long train, which besides being more romantic, is more suitable for an evening wedding.

These two brides display the range of variation between contemporary* (left) *and traditional* (right) *dress.

Choosing the Season

Here are some factors you may want to consider before deciding on your wedding date:

SUMMERTIME
- is generally the best time for an outdoor wedding.
- also brings the hot weather.
- holds the possibility of conflicting vacation times.
- is a popular wedding season and may present scheduling difficulties.

AUTUMN
- provides cool, crisp weather.
- offers more scheduling options.
- is also a time for college commitments.

WINTER
- is ideal for a cozy indoor wedding.
- is a romantic time of year.
- also means unpredictable weather.
- coincides with the busy holiday season.

SPRING
- is appropriate for weddings and new beginnings.
- is traditionally associated with love.
- can provide lovely (if somewhat unpredictable) weather.

A wedding pair,* le beau idéal, *are chic and good-looking, and very much attired in the prevailing haute fashion.

truly an elusive ingredient not universally subscribed to in every respect. It is personal, unique. The bride's wedding gown, whether long or short, traditional or modern, must fit appropriately and be made of stylish and unobtrusive fabric. A full-length gown is more suitable for evening and formal ceremonies. A veil and train give greater formality to the bride's gown. For daytime, or informal weddings, shorter dresses, even pastel colors, can be appropriate. Inevitably brides carry either a spray of flowers or wear a corsage.

Makeup ought to be on the light side. Besides creating a tasteful approach to one's appearance, it helps to enhance the photographs.

The bride's dress will set the styles of all the other women present—bridesmaids, maid of honor, and the mothers of the bride and the groom. All their gowns, whatever the materials—silk, taffeta, or organza—should coordinate with shoes or slippers.

The choice of outfits for the men in the wedding party should complement the women's. No matter what the decision, there are many choices: formal, which requires dinner jackets, cutaway coats and trousers, ascots, silk hats, or informal, which requires just plain, old-fashioned business suits. What counts is what's appropriate for the occasion.

Except for large political or social weddings, in which display of wealth and trappings are paramount considerations, most weddings today minimize pretentious excess. It has been estimated that a modestly budgeted wedding runs to ten thousand dollars, which isn't inexpensive, but it doesn't allow for extravagant expenditures.

Pinched at the waist, her dress also exhibits a high collar. The groom wears an Oxford gray cutaway coat, trousers, vest, and ascot; he has dispensed with a gray silk top hat.

Andrea Wilkin's "Ricarda" is a gown of silk georgette with antique lace that sweeps to the ground in three tiers. The bride's head remains uncovered in this antique look.

This groom complements his bride perfectly. He is bedecked in an Yves Saint Laurent black single-breasted tuxedo that is most appropriate for a formal evening ceremony.

Here is a headdress and veil with lines and materials that coordinate perfectly with the dress.

Alfred Angelo's luxurious gown is the epitome of romantic allure, with abundant lace and organza. Notice the bouquet wrapped in matching organza.

Military Wedding Etiquette

Before taking steps in planning a military ceremony, consult the groom's commanding officer and/or the official hostess at any military academy for details and procedures. Remember that the wedding invitations will differ in how the groom's title is treated. For junior officers, the branch of service and rank appear below the name, while senior officers state their rank as their title.

One of the most dramatic and memorable aspects of the military wedding is the arch of sabers (army) or swords (navy). As the wedding party leaves the church, the head usher will give the command to "draw" the weapons for the newly married couple to pass beneath. He then commands the "return" of the weapons as the rest of the bridal party passes through.

This bride's simple headpiece and veil accentuate the intricate detailing of the bodice of her gown. She has kept her make-up light so that her portrait looks perfect.

The floral overlay completes the decorative Indian marriage dress for both the bride and her groom. Natural elements play an important role in any outdoor ceremony—Eastern- or Western-style.

The formal Mexican wedding displays clothes that are based on traditional costume. The bride and groom here, in a Catholic ceremony, are wed by their local priest.

This couple displays clothing from the American South, a style dating from the mid-nineteenth century.

A Muslim couple from Malay, regally adorned, are seated on their wedding throne in a Singapore mosque.

This beautiful gown goes for the details. It is made of duchess satin with hand-beaded details on the bodice, skirt, and sleeves.

Here is a groom in full black dress, from After Six. His attire is well-chosen for a formal wedding ceremony.

"Primrose," in gray satin, is also available in white or ivory.

The floor-length veil shown above is customarily worn only at a formal wedding that will take place in the evening.

This fingertip veil is one that can be worn for a formal or informal wedding, day or evening.

The Jewish Wedding

The Jewish wedding is a service that dates from the tribes of ancient Israel, but incorporates many religious ingredients that the Jews have acquired in the lands in which they have settled. Wedding services vary among the orthodox, conservative, and reformed congregations—whether taking place in Chicago, Tel Aviv, Buenos Aires, or Calcutta—but the substance is the same. With the exception of the orthodox ceremony, where professional go-betweens may bring together a suitable groom with an available bride, couples meet freely in social situations.

All Jewish services take place under the bridal canopy, chuppah.

The site for the wedding may be a synagogue, which offers sacred surroundings, or it may take place at the bride's home. Reformed Jews often rent hotel ballrooms or community centers that can accommodate a large number of guests for the ceremony and the reception. And alternatively, weddings are often held outdoors, on a lawn or in a garden. Occasionally a wedding is planned during the summer, at night, under starry skies.

Although it is the legal, traditional right of any Jew to perform a wedding service, almost all Jewish weddings are conducted by rabbis.

Inasmuch as the purpose of the marriage is to establish a home, the ceremony takes place under a floral canopy, a symbolic "roof," called a chuppah. *More specifically, the* chuppah *symbolizes the bridal chamber and the move of the bride from her father's home to the new one of her husband. Sometimes a blue cloth is used to cover the roof of the canopy, which is representative of the heavens above, a prod to the couple, so it is said, to elevate themselves spiritually.*

With the couple before him, the rabbi invokes the benediction over a cup of wine, conveying a sacred compact between God and man, and honoring the marriage as a holy ritual. The couple drinks from the cup, and the groom places the ring on his bride's left forefinger, reciting, "Thou art consecrated unto me with this ring as my wife, according to the law of Moses and Israel, and the State of..."

The ceremony concludes when the groom breaks his glass under his heel, a symbolic reminder of the destruction of the Temple in Jerusalem and the dispersion of Israel. Under the chuppah *the newlyweds welcome their guests. (Reformed Jews consider the traditional* chuppah *an optional wedding ingredient in the United States, along with the crushing of the bridegroom's glass.)*

After toasting the couple with wine or champagne, the feast begins. Later there is social dancing. Among the orthodox, the men and women dance separately, often in different rooms. The music may be comprised of anything from tradi-

tional European folk songs to the Israeli "Hora," to show tunes from Fiddler on the Roof. *Sometimes the ceremony will include traditional ritualistic dances, when the guests dance around the bride, the men snapping their fingers, clapping their hands, and kicking their heels in the air.*

This happy bride enjoys the traditional dancing and festivities at her wedding reception.

A blessing over the bread* (challah) *is recited to signal the start of the post-ceremony meal.

Religious Restrictions for the Wedding Date

If you wish to have a religious ceremony, you will want to know about religious rules that will affect your choice of the wedding date. If you are Christian, you cannot marry on holy days such as Easter and Christmas. Roman Catholics should note that no marriage can take place during the holy week. Jewish doctrine allows no marriages on the Sabbath and on high holy days.

In all cases, a minister, priest, or rabbi should be consulted.

A New England Wedding

The original non-native Americans were the Yankees, those first settlers of New England who were known for resourcefulness, ingenuity, and thrift. The raw, harsh climate of the Massachusetts colony exaggerated the importance of an homogenized faith, sometimes exhibiting an intolerance for beliefs that were at variance with churchly, Puritanical views. Those weddings were under the supervision of the state, although the ceremony itself followed the strictures of the religious ceremony.

In the eighteenth century the bride customarily chose the text for the sermon that would be delivered on the Sunday she became a bride. She and her husband-to-be anxiously searched for long hours through the family Bible for the appropriate text. The "Song of Solomon" almost always offered a suitable sentiment for the occasion.

The "coming-out," or "walking out," of the bride and groom was an important event in the community. The couple usually led a procession of five or six couples on their way to the church, an event that was observed by the entire town and meeting house.

A wedding in an unadorned New England meeting house. The plain interior is classically beautiful and provides a picture-perfect setting.

Sometimes the bride and groom would take prominent seats in the church gallery and during the sermon rise to their feet, turning about several times slowly, in an effort to show their bridal finery to the admiring congregation.

The wedding cake and bridal gloves were usually sent to relatives and friends of both families. In anticipation of the impending wedding, the couple would publish their banns three times in the meeting house during a town meeting, a public lecture, or a Sunday service. It was customary for the Town Clerk, the deacon, or the minister at any of these events to read off the names of the contracting parties. A notice, additionally, was placed on the church's door, or on a so-called "publishing post."

A look at contemporary New England weddings discloses no surprises. Weddings are no longer grounded in the intolerance of the Puritan church, but instead follow the tradition of the major religious sects that, as immigrants, settled New England in the two hundred years that have elapsed since then. Catholic, Protestant, Jewish, and Eastern Orthodox rituals prevail, following, with minor variations, their traditional ceremonies. Alternatively, civil services continue to be performed in city halls and municipal centers, conducted by magistrates or laymen of ecumenical turns-of-mind.

An antique horse-drawn buggy is an innovative choice for the honeymoon getaway vehicle at this New England wedding, which took place in a landmark home.

Wedding Sizes

Finances and the tone you want to set for your wedding—lively and elaborate or intimate and cozy—will best determine the most appropriate wedding size for you. Small, medium, and large weddings all have their special features. A small guest list will lend itself well to an intimate church, club, or home setting. At the reception you will be able to mingle and converse freely with close friends and relatives. The smaller wedding also allows for extra creativity and freedom in choosing the site for the ceremony and reception, since presumably you are better acquainted with your guests and their tastes. And the smaller wedding gives you more of a feeling of control over the events and lessens your nervousness, which is an important factor on your wedding day.

The large guest list complements a church- or cathedral-size wedding, and is also recommended for a ceremony in a hotel with a large ballroom. It allows you to invite everyone you wish and eliminates the family bickering over who to invite. A big wedding is a wonderful setting for dancing and merrymaking among guests, and it guarantees fun, wonderful memories, and plenty of diverse photographs. The larger guest list seems to create more of everything, including presents, bills, and thank-you notes. Of course, you can always opt for a medium-size wedding and enjoy a combination of the advantages.

Linens and Bundling

It took nearly a thousand years for weddings to go public. Couples would let their families know they had chosen their mates and that they wanted to get married. They would then publicize their intentions in publishing the banns in church, which was a public declaration of their intentions and choice of mate.

The service began outside the church and ended inside with a bridal mass. Until the twelfth century priests did not participate in the service; although church authorities did recognize the marriage when it took place, it was considered legal. When the church finally took charge of weddings and blessed them in solemnly conducted services, for the first time lines of inheritance were fixed, and children born of the marriage were legally identified.

Should the bridal couple plan a night party in a conservatory after the wedding, here is an unusual display of the grand style in which to do it.

At the time of the Reformation, the state replaced the church in offering legal shelter for the marriage, thus introducing the secular wedding. In New England, the puritan minister was frequently replaced by a civil magistrate. Couples who wanted to get married were obliged to announce their intentions at three public meetings. When youths came to the colonies from England they were expected to present good character references from someone in authority from their hometowns. It was expected that the men were free of "any amatory entanglements" before they were permitted to freely pay court to any of the local women.

Because women's rights in the New England home were diminished under the influence of puritan theologists and these women were sometimes overshadowed by domineering mothers-in-law, women found increased emancipation by settling on the frontier. Working alongside fathers, husbands, and brothers, these working conditions gave them higher, more equal, social status and dignity than that of their sisters in New England.

Courtship in bitter cold New England involved some innovations when it came to interpersonal relations. When a young man chose a young woman he wished to become acquainted with, he asked her parents' permission to pay her a visit. Should the weather be prohibitive for the return to his home, and the distance considerable, the youth might be permitted to remain with the woman and her family overnight. When the woman's parents retired to a bed in a corner of the room, the woman and her gentleman caller would "bundle" together in her bed, frequently in the same room as her parents. The couple remained dressed in their underclothing while covered up to their necks in furs and down comforters. Thus they remained warm and had an opportunity to "neck" to their heart's delight. As far as the woman's parents were concerned, they were perfectly satisfied that their daughter's night of "larking" was proper. They had

A splendidly stylish collection of bedroom furnishings—today's version of the bundling accouterments. "Rose Moss" is hand-stencilled in a spectrum of colors onto moiré, a silk fabric. Pillows and coverlet can be used in concert or, sprinkled throughout a house, as accents.

Harrod's of London created this rather decadent display of their most elegant satin bed linens.

Perfect gifts are table linens from a garden in Sussex, England, that would work in any newlyweds' garden worldwide.

From the Laura Ashley Dining Collection, these small details that enhance married life make perfect wedding gifts.

suitably, after all, chaperoned the couple, who may have either decided to "plight their troth," or never to see each other again, during the interlude. As an additional safeguard against sexual temptation in a Puritan home, the woman's parents would position a long board, fitted with slots, between the couple. Although a naive device serving to frustrate passionate embraces during the night, it could not inhibit the contact of straying hands and lips.

An alternative to "bundling" in colonial days was the use of a six-foot hollowed-out tube, fitted with a mouth and earpiece. This device was employed as a means of private and intimate conversation by passionate couples in the midst of a family gathering. It was all quite proper as they would sit opposite each other, whispering into the tube. No one in the room considered their behavior rude nor paid them any attention.

Today the closest approximation of the original bundling is the importance that linens play in the overall wedding preparations: as important and usable gifts for the couple after their wedding. It is no small coincidence that the nuptial bed is represented by the giving of linens or that they are a primary focus of the couple's acquisitions if they are not received as gifts.

Couples may not "bundle" in the New England sense today, but linens, particularly bed linens, are a primary element of every wedding—whether formal or casual—in that they represent the major change in the relationship between being engaged and "wedded."

The Russian Wedding

The Russian Eastern Orthodox church flourishes in a number of communities outside the Soviet Union as though Soviet atheism and the revolution never happened. At the root of its faith is the belief in the everlasting ideal of Mother Russia, who, with the Czar at its head, constitutes the family-nation and the foundation of the church. There is a surviving adoration of the saints, the liturgy, and the icon art (the sacred images of Jesus and Mary) of Byzantine Russia in many ceremonies.

Today when Russian couples marry outside the Soviet Union they are wed in a church of Byzantine architecture, before an altar where the priest intones the ancient service while holding crowns above the heads of the bride and groom. The bride sips ceremonial wine, and the couple drinks three times from the same cup—the cup of experience—symbolizing their desire to comingle their lives.

Today the Soviet wedding ceremony in Russia is a civil service, a businesslike affair with no religious overtones. Religious beliefs are considered a private affair; marriage is a State concern.

But brides and grooms there, as everywhere else, want to celebrate their wedding with more than institutional tolerance. They give vent to a normal newlyweds' glow: celebrating with friends. In addition to libations, food, and iced champagne, they participate in a particular ritual, by driving about the city, visiting important monuments. This might be done in a decorated private car, or in a "wedding taxi," which carries two identifying rings on its roof. It is not uncommon for the couple to toss their empty champagne bottles into a river, or for the bride to skim her bridal crown onto the water.

On some occasions groups of couples get married before the same state clerk and celebrate their unions together.

Even without all the fanfare habitual to Western-style weddings, young Russian couples have found some distinctive methods to celebrate their weddings creatively.

When a couple weds in the Soviet Union, one standard tradition is for the newlyweds and their guests to tour the city's major sights. Thus, most Russian wedding portraits include a picture of the bride and groom at a historic site. Shown here is a typical private vehicle at a Moscow wedding, decorated as a wedding car.

This Soviet wedding party is about to embark on a traditional Volga River cruise. The wedding group may not only travel by car, but may also cruise a major waterway.

Recommended Wedding Photos

BEFORE THE WEDDING:
- Bridal portrait
- Bride dressing
- Bride with parents
- Bride leaving home
- Bride with attendants
- Bride with siblings
- Groom dressing
- Groom leaving home

KEY ASPECTS OF THE WEDDING CEREMONY:
- Procession and recession
- Exchange of vows
- Ring ceremony

AT THE RECEPTION:
- Newly married couple arriving
- The receiving line
- Table of honor
- Parents' table
- The key dances
- The best man's toast
- Cake cutting and eating
- Garter throwing
- Bouquet throwing
- Newly married couple leaving for honeymoon

Always let the photographer know what special pictures you want, and decide which photos should be in color and which in black and white. Get to know the photographer before the wedding to make sure he or she is right for your wedding style.

The married Soviet couple, following their civil ceremony before a magistrate, signs their license.

Throwing Shoes

The old-fashioned act of tossing old shoes into the path of the bridal couple or tying shoes to the rear of their car, comes from the rather primitive belief that the newlyweds must repel the evil-eye, or demons, before they start their life together. It's for luck, to begin on the very best of terms with the magical powers "out there."

Shoes have always had an immense psychological importance in fairy tales. They take on magical characteristics. The familiar fairy tale of Cinderella, with the importance of the Prince finding her lost slipper and going in search of the one who has "possessed" it, makes this point clearly. Another view of the same gesture is that old shoes symbolize possession of one person by the other—probably the female to the male, in prefeminist terms.

The old shoes, in a sense, represent the bride's father. When they are tossed in the direction of the newlyweds, it is symbolic of the father relinquishing his authority, his rights, over his daughter.

The traditional reason for the honeymoon was that because of the waning nature of the passion of newlyweds, like the waning moon, a time should be set aside for a period of time when the couple can have complete privacy. Obviously

After a June wedding in a Maine church garden, these newlyweds drive off in a four-wheeled carriage—to the applause of their guests.

Honeymoons tend to encourage unorthodox escape routes. Although many couples depart by plane, in this case the groom is also the pilot.

this is not only a time for uninhibited romance, but for solitude, relaxation, and escape to a secluded rendezvous, out-of-reach of intruding, well-meaning families and friends. The word "honeymoon" derives from the German flitterwochen, *which literally means tinsel weeks, a time of glitter.*

The honeymoon is a post-nuptial event that has survived from days when many a bride was kidnapped by the groom who was disguised and carried her off to a secret hiding place to avoid the wrath of her father. With the passage of time, the couple sought a reconciliation with the bride's father by wooing him with dazzling gifts.

Today it isn't only shoes that are tied to the departing nuptial vehicle; in fact, it is probably an item other than shoes that will start the couple on the road to a happy life. Some cars are decorated with cans, others with balloons or streamers, and yet others with just flowers.

In addition, the couple will not necessarily depart in the original manner, by horsecart—although some couples choose to follow this tradition strictly. More likely, the couple will leave in a car that has been outfitted for the occasion.

The Recordkeeper

By Lily Laketon

Introduction

Now that you've decided to get married, your wedding day promises to be the most important day of all. You will want everything—from your dress to the music to the flowers to the food—to be perfect. But when you come down to earth, you'll see there's a lot of practical planning that must take place.

If you're like most brides, you'll find planning the wedding fun—but also time-consuming, exhausting, and, at times, troublesome. Not only do you have to start from scratch—deciding on the place and time of the ceremony and reception, choosing a menu, hiring a photographer, picking your maids (and their dresses, along with yours)—but you have to anticipate troubles along the way.

That's where this wedding planner helps. In it there's space to record the planning details of your wedding that you'll need to keep track of. After all, the more organized your wedding planning is, the easier it will be.

The most important things to keep in mind?

• *Allow ample time. Almost everything taskes longer than you think—and having some extra time will prevent problems. With enough time, your bangs can grow out by the wedding day, your dress can be sent back for more alterations, you can get every single reply card back in the mail.*

• *Double check all details. Even if you said "buttercream," the baker might have heard "butterscotch." So be sure to reconfirm all times, places, dates, amounts, etc., and be sure that all the professionals you're working with are doing things to your exact specifications.*

- *Be willing to compromise when necessary. If the maid's dress you like just doesn't come in magenta, you may have to take rosebud pink instead—or choose another style that does come in magenta. This doesn't mean you should settle for anything that isn't to your liking. It just means that you should know when it would be better to find an alternative.*
- *Compare costs. Everything these days is expensive. But if you don't have a particular preference—for a photographer, say, or for certain types of flowers, or for a main course of lobster—then shop around and choose the best buy for your money.*
- *Write down everything. Keep track not only of the times of all appointments but all the details too. There are so many items to think about. If you're sure to write them all down, you'll always have the information when and where you need it.*

Above all, keep your sense of humor. Everyone is bound to have some disagreements—with parents, friends, attendants, even your fiancé. If a problem seems overwhelming, discuss it later, when you've all calmed down—or when the problem no longer seems so serious.

But don't think that wedding planning is full of problems! It can be an exciting, joyous time—especially since it will culminate with your wedding.

So start filling in the following pages as soon as you're engaged. For specific questions, consult an etiquette book or ask your bridal consultant, clergyman, photographer, florist, etc.

In the meantime, let the fun begin. Happy planning, happy wedding, and, most of all, happy ever after.

Planning Schedule

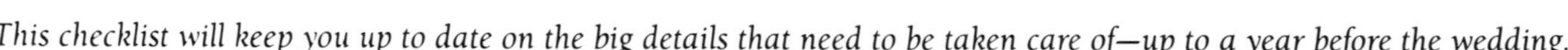

This checklist will keep you up to date on the big details that need to be taken care of—up to a year before the wedding.

SIX MONTHS TO ONE YEAR BEFORE

- [ ] Decide on the date, time, and place of your wedding—and make reservations (early!) for the church, synagogue, and reception hall.
- [ ] Discuss your wedding budget with your fiancé and with everyone who's chipping in—your parents, maybe his parents too.
- [ ] Send announcement to local newspapers.
- [ ] Draw up a tentative guest list.
- [ ] Make the reservations for caterer, musicians, clergyman, florist, photographer.
- [ ] Go shopping for your wedding dress, veil, and accessories.
- [ ] With your fiancé, pick out your engagement ring, if you haven't already.
- [ ] Register at the wedding gift registry of your favorite department and specialty stores for all the things you'll need—china, tableware, linens, and other house necessities.
- [ ] Choose your bridesmaids, groomsmen, and honor attendants. Select dresses for maids.
- [ ] Get sizes for members of the wedding party.
- [ ] Start making honeymoon plans; reserve tickets and hotel rooms ahead of time.

THREE TO SIX MONTHS BEFORE

- [ ] Order wedding invitations (and announcements, if you plan to send them to those who aren't invited to the wedding).
- [ ] Firm up the guest list.
- [ ] Order outfits—if you're renting them—for the groom and the groomsmen.
- [ ] Experiment with your wedding hairstyle, so there's time for your hair to grow out.
- [ ] Order wedding flowers, including bouquets, corsages, and boutonnieres.
- [ ] Make reservations with the photographer and schedule an appointment for your wedding portrait.
- [ ] Confirm reservations for your honeymoon and buy travel tickets.

ONE MONTH BEFORE

- ☐ Address and mail wedding invitations.
- ☐ Order your wedding cake, if it's not included with the catered meal.
- ☐ Buy gifts for all your attendants.
- ☐ Choose your wedding ring and your groom's, if he'll have one.
- ☐ Reserve lodgings for out-of-town attendants—maybe at a local hotel.
- ☐ Help plan your rehearsal dinner along with the groom's family or the relatives or friends who are giving it for you.
- ☐ Send your wedding announcement to the society page of the local newspaper.
- ☐ Write thank-you notes for the gifts that have already arrived.
- ☐ Start planning the bachelor's party and the bridesmaids' luncheon.
- ☐ Discuss with the photographer any special photos you'd like taken—you can even give him a list of can't-be-missed shots.
- ☐ Prepare your traveling clothes for the honeymoon. Buy things you'll need but don't already have.
- ☐ Arrange for any changes of name and address.

ONE WEEK BEFORE

- ☐ Start packing for your honeymoon.
- ☐ Address wedding announcements so they're ready to mail immediately after the wedding, and give them to a family member or friend to mail.
- ☐ Hold the rehearsal dinner (a day or two in advance of the wedding). Be sure you've notified all participants of the time and place.
- ☐ Give the caterer an estimate of the number of guests.
- ☐ Reconfirm all ceremony and reception details—with the caterer, musicians, clergyman, florist, photographer, etc.
- ☐ Continue writing thank-you notes.
- ☐ Start moving into your new home.

Wedding Budget

Even if your parents are footing the bill for your wedding, you'll want to help them come up with a cost estimate—and to work with them so you all can get the most for your money. Traditionally the bride's family pays for nearly all the wedding costs—invitations, the bride's outfit, flowers, photographs, and rental of the ceremony site and the reception, including all food and entertainment. The groom or his family pays for the bride's wedding and engagement rings, the marriage license, the clergyman's fee, and the honeymoon. Attendants usually buy or rent their own outfits.

Use this list to keep track of estimated and actual wedding expenses.

STATIONERY	ESTIMATED COST	ACTUAL COST
Invitations		
Announcements		
Enclosures (maps, reply cards)		
Thank-you notes		

FLOWERS	ESTIMATED COST	ACTUAL COST
Ceremony flowers		
Bride's bouquets		
Attendants' bouquets		
Corsages for mothers		
Boutonnieres for men		
Reception centerpieces		
Other reception flowers		

RECEPTION	ESTIMATED COST	ACTUAL COST
Transportation		
Decorations		
Cake		
Food		
Liquor		
Waiters and bartender		

MUSIC	ESTIMATED COST	ACTUAL COST
Organist		
Soloist		
Reception band		

PHOTOGRAPHY	ESTIMATED COST	ACTUAL COST
Engagement portrait		
Wedding portrait		
Wedding candids		
Extra prints		

BRIDE'S OUTFIT	ESTIMATED COST	ACTUAL COST
Dress		
Headpiece and veil		
Shoes		
Lingerie		
Accessories		

GIFTS	ESTIMATED COST	ACTUAL COST
For attendants		
For groom		
Groom's wedding ring		

Guest List

It would be great if you could invite everybody you know to your wedding. But you'll probably be constrained by space (the reception site has to be able to accommodate all your guests comfortably) and price. The easiest way to pare down the guest list? Eliminate, if you must, children, business friends, distant cousins, and people who live far away. You might also limit the number of guests from each of your families.

This list holds space for 150 families of individuals—and when you've filled in all their addresses, you'll have them all at hand when you address the wedding invitations. (You can use this list, too, for thank-you notes, since only those who attend the reception are expected to send gifts.)

NAME & ADDRESS	NUMBER ATTENDING	WILL NOT ATTEND

NAME ADDRESS	NUMBER ATTENDING	WILL NOT ATTEND

NAME & ADDRESS	NUMBER ATTENDING	WILL NOT ATTEND

NAME & ADDRESS	NUMBER ATTENDING	WILL NOT ATTEND

Wedding Announcements

You may want to send printed announcements that includes your new address to those who couldn't be invited to the wedding, but whom you'd like to know about your marriage. Ask your printer about wording at the same time you order invitations. Have announcements addressed, stamped, and ready to send immediately after the wedding.

WEDDING ANNOUNCEMENT WORDING:

PEOPLE TO SEND WEDDING ANNOUNCEMENTS TO:

NAME & ADDRESS

NAME & ADDRESS

NAME & ADDRESS

Newspaper Announcement

You'll undoubtedly want notice of your wedding to appear in your local newspaper. What information to include? Check the style of your paper to see. Often it's this:

- ☐ Your name, your parents, their hometown (sometimes your grandparents)
- ☐ Your fiancé's name, his parents, their hometown (sometimes his grandparents)
- ☐ Time and place of wedding and reception
- ☐ Attendants and their hometowns
- ☐ Educational background of you and your fiancé

- ☐ Professions of you and your fiancé
- ☐ Your parents' professions
- ☐ Your fiancé's parents' professions
- ☐ Description of your dress and bouquet
- ☐ Description of your attendants' dresses and bouquets
- ☐ Honeymoon plans

Submit the information on your newspaper's standard form, or type it out yourself. Be sure to include your name, address, and telephone number (for verification). If you'd like a photo published, include a black-and-white 8 × 10 glossy.

ANNOUNCEMENT WORDING:

Planning with the Pros

Keep an easy-to-refer-to list of all the professionals you'll need to be in touch with during the planning, and jot down under "notes" any information you should keep track of. Always check and recheck all details. It's a good idea to keep a planning calendar, too, for appointments and delivery dates.

CLERGYMAN	DATES & TIMES OF APPOINTMENTS	NOTES
Name		
Address & Phone		

ORGANIST	DATES & TIMES OF APPOINTMENTS	NOTES
Name		
Address & Phone		

SOLOIST	DATES & TIMES OF APPOINTMENTS	NOTES
Name		
Address & Phone		

PRINTER	DATES & TIMES OF APPOINTMENTS	NOTES
Name		
Address & Phone		

FLORIST	DATES & TIMES OF APPOINTMENTS	NOTES
Name		
Address & Phone		

PHOTOGRAPHER	DATES & TIMES OF APPOINTMENTS	NOTES
Name		
Address & Phone		

CATERER	DATES & TIMES OF APPOINTMENTS	NOTES
Name		
Address & Phone		

BAKER	DATES & TIMES OF APPOINTMENTS	NOTES
Name		
Address & Phone		

MUSICIANS	DATES & TIMES OF APPOINTMENTS	NOTES
Name		
Address & Phone		

OTHER	DATES & TIMES OF APPOINTMENTS	NOTES
Name		
Address & Phone		

OTHER	DATES & TIMES OF APPOINTMENTS	NOTES
Name		
Address & Phone		

OTHER	DATES & TIMES OF APPOINTMENTS	NOTES
Name		
Address & Phone		

OTHER	DATES & TIMES OF APPOINTMENTS	NOTES
Name		
Address & Phone		

Wedding Invitations

Your printer will be able to show you the traditional invitation wording—but don't hesitate to use your own words. Write your invitation wording here, exactly as it should appear.

Number of invitations? You'll need one for every married couple, one for every single adult guest. Order a few extras as souvenirs, to keep among your memorabilia.

Be sure to get a sample invitation so you can check for the following: correct wording, correct spellings of all names, correct spellings of all places, correct day and date, complete addresses.

What else might you need? Reply cards, maps if the guests won't know how to get to the ceremony or reception site, maybe even matching stationery for thank-you notes.

WEDDING INVITATION WORDING:

Flowers

What flowers will you need? Bouquets, of course, for you and your maids, boutonnieres for the men in the wedding party, corsages for mothers and special guests. Besides that, you'll want to decorate the ceremony and reception sites. Choose multicolored flowers or those that match your wedding color scheme. Keep in mind the time of year, too—flowers in season are likely to be less expensive.

CEREMONY	KINDS OF FLOWERS	COLOR	NUMBER
Altar			
Pews			
Aisles			
Other			

WEDDING PARTY	KINDS OF FLOWERS	COLOR	NUMBER
Bride			
Maid of honor			
Bridesmaids			
Flower girl			
Mother of the bride			
Mother of the groom			
Other female relatives or friends			
Father of the bride			
Father of the groom			
Best man			
Groomsmen			
Ring bearer			
Other male relatives or friends			

RECEPTION FLOWERS	KINDS OF FLOWERS	COLOR	NUMBER
Bride's table			
Parents' table			
Cake table			
Guest tables			
Other			

The Wedding Cake

Your cake might be included in the catering fee—or you can order it separately. Choose any flavor you love—and maybe have your names and the date written on top! You might want a groom's cake too—traditionally it's a dark-colored cake or a fruit-cake packaged in individual boxes for female guests to take home, put under their pillows, supposedly provoking dreams of future husbands!

Size	
Number to serve	
Shape	
Cake flavor	
Filling flavor	
Frosting flavor	
Frosting color	
Inscription on top	

Decorative topper	
Other decorations	

Groom's cake flavor	
Frosting flavor	
Number of boxes	
Decorations on boxes	

Your Wedding Dress

Your wedding dress ought to be the most beautiful dress you've ever worn. Your best bet before shopping? Thumb through some bridal magazines to get an idea of the styles you like the most. Then go shopping, maybe with your mother or a friend.

WRITE DOWN ALL THE NECESSARY INFORMATION HERE.

Bridal salon/Consultant's name	
Dress	
Headpiece	
Shoes	
Lingerie	
Gloves/Hose	
Jewelry	
Fittings	Pick up

Attendants' Dresses 

Since your attendants will be paying for their own dresses, you may want to consult with them before making a final decision. Try to pick dresses they can wear later for other occasions, and look for a style that will look right on people of different shapes and sizes.

MAID OF HONOR

Style	
Color	
Size	
Accessories	

MAID

Style	
Color	
Size	
Accessories	

MAID

Style	
Color	
Size	
Accessories	

MAID

Style	
Color	
Size	
Accessories	

MAID

Style	
Color	
Size	
Accessories	

MAID

Style	
Color	
Size	
Accessories	

Men's Wedding Clothes

Your fiancé will probably be renting his outfit from a formalwear shop and having it fitted a few days before the wedding. Ask all male attendants, as well as your father and your fiance's father, for their sizes—they'll need to be fitted too. Extras like vests, suspenders, cuff links, and ties are included—and you can even rent shoes.

Wedding Showers

Showers are given by bridal attendants or close friends of yours—and any setting, any type of party at all will do. The main focus? Opening the gifts, of course. Be sure to keep track of all gifts you receive—so you can send thank-you notes.

SHOWER THEME: HOSTESS:

Address Date

GUEST	GIFT	DATE OF THANK-YOU NOTE

SHOWER THEME: HOSTESS:

Address Date

GUEST	GIFT	DATE OF THANK-YOU NOTE

SHOWER THEME: HOSTESS:

Address Date

GUEST	GIFT	DATE OF THANK-YOU NOTE

Wedding Gifts

The gifts you give will be to your attendants (your fiancé will give gifts to his groomsmen).

The gifts you receive will be from all guests who attend the reception. Gifts will probably be brought or sent to your home before the wedding. Be sure to keep cards with gifts so you know what came from whom.

WEDDING GIFT LIST

FROM	GIFT	PURCHASED AT	DATE RECEIVED	THANK-YOU SENT

FROM	GIFT	PURCHASED AT	DATE RECEIVED	THANK-YOU SENT

FROM	GIFT	PURCHASED AT	DATE RECEIVED	THANK-YOU SENT

FROM	GIFT	PURCHASED AT	DATE RECEIVED	THANK-YOU SENT

Pointers

On the day of the wedding, be sure to allow plenty of time for preparing so everything goes as smoothly as possible. You and your attendants should start dressing about two hours before the ceremony. Following that, you can have some pictures taken. Groomsmen should be at the ceremony site about thirty to fourty-five minutes before the ceremony so they can seat guests as they begin to arrive. If the wedding is large, you can omit the men from the receiving line—or you can omit all attendants except the maid of honor and the best man.

Here's the traditional order for the procession:

Clergyman; Groom; Best man; (They will be at the altar, awaiting the rest of the wedding party.) Groomsmen and bridesmaids, in pairs (or groomsmen in pairs precede bridesmaids in pairs); Maid of honor; Ring bearer and flower girl; Bride and her father.

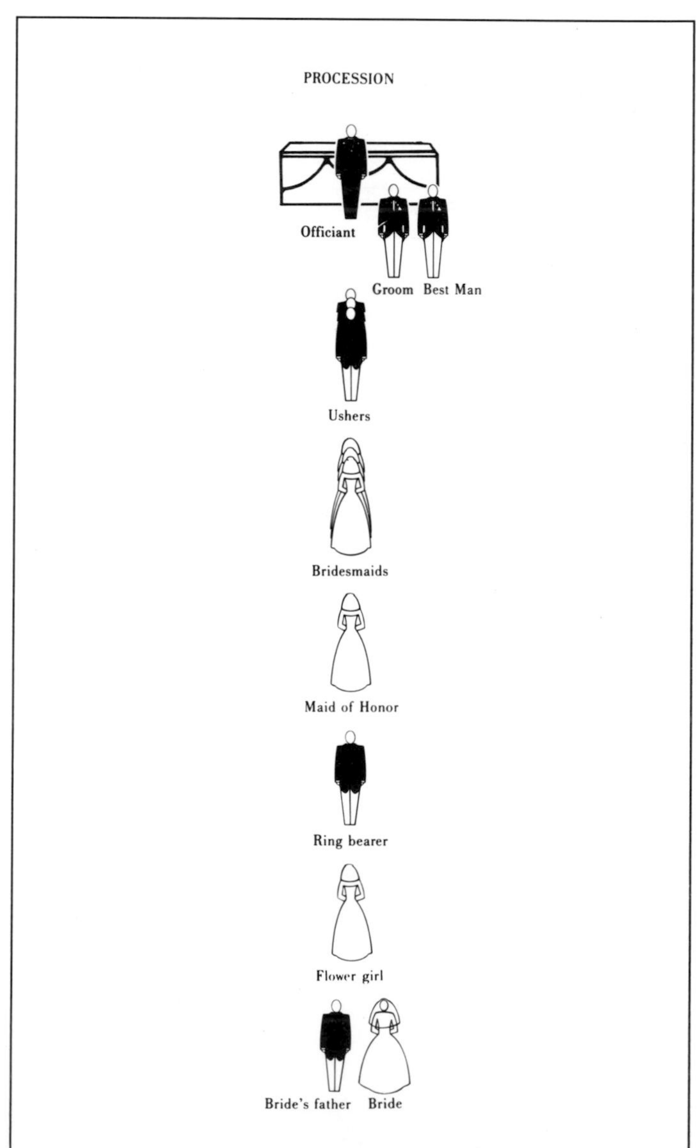

Here's the order for the recession:

Bride and groom; Flower girl and ring bearer; Maid of honor and best man; Bridesmaids and groomsmen, in pairs.

Immediately after the ceremony, or as guests enter the reception area, you'll form the receiving line so you can give all guests a personal greeting.

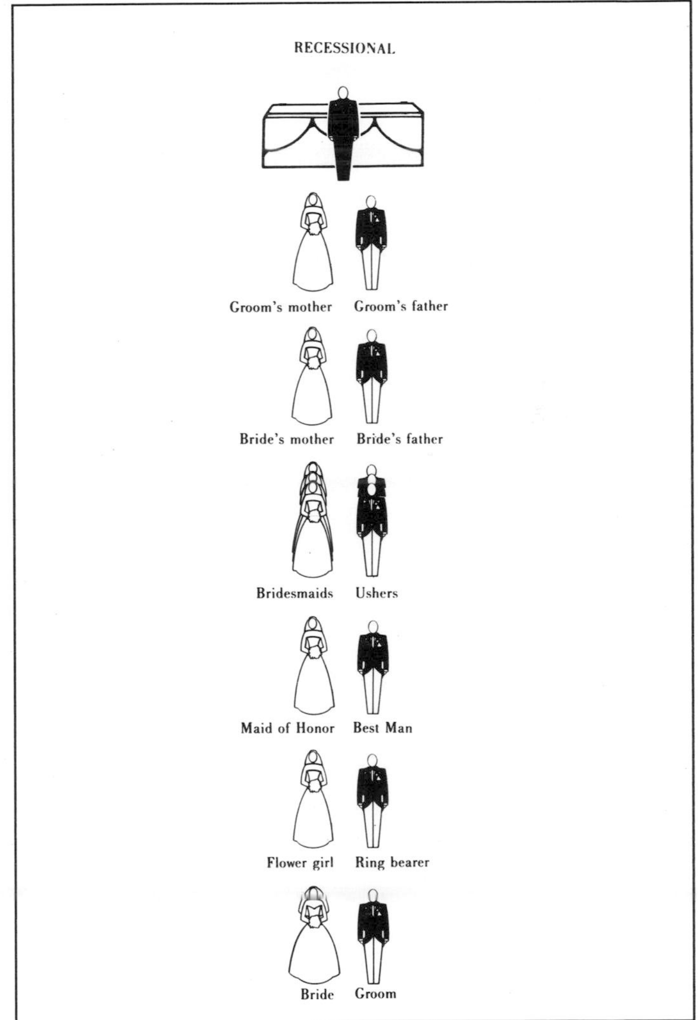

Here's the order of the receiving line.

Bride's mother; Bride's father; Groom's mother; Groom's father; Bride; Groom; Maid of honor; Best man; Bridesmaids; Groomsmen.

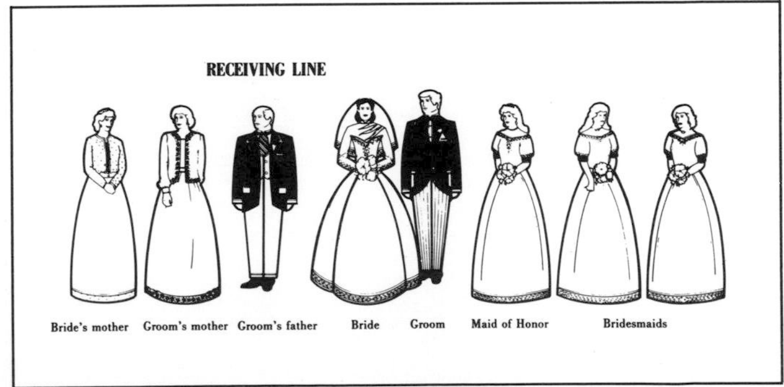

Reception

The wedding ceremony is not the only tradition-filled rite on your wedding day—the reception also has a number of traditions all its own. The customary seating arrangement?

There are two tables. The bride's table includes the bride, the groom, and their attendants, with bridesmaids and groomsmen seated alternately.

The parents' table includes all parents, the clergyman and his wife, grandparents, and other especially close relatives.

Of course, you can vary the seating arrangements to your liking, depending on the shape and size of the tables. Or you can have more than one parents' table for different sides of the family or if parents are divorced.

FIRST DANCE

You and your groom will start off the dancing with the traditional "first dance." If you feel shy about having the spotlight on you while you're dancing, ask your father to cut in quickly.

The dance order—traditional but optional—goes like this:

Bride and groom

Bride and her father/Groom and bride's mother

Bride and best man/Groom and maid of honor

Bride and groom's father/Groom and groom's mother

Then maids, groomsmen, and other guests will join in. (The groom and all groomsmen should take their turns dancing with all the bridesmaids, too.)

TOAST AND CAKE CUTTING

Hand over hand, you and your groom will cut the cake, feeding each other a bite of the first slice. Then the caterer or a friend can take over. When all guests have a piece of cake, the best man proposes a toast—to you, your groom, anyone else he'd like to include. (Relatives and other guests can reply to the toast or propose more toasts of their own.)

BOUQUET AND GARTER THROWING

These take place just before you leave the reception, with the woman who catches the bouquet and the man who catches the garter the next to marry, of course. After you change and bid your parents good-bye, it's off to the honeymoon—in a shower of rice!

Your Honeymoon

It should be the most romantic trip of your life! But your honeymoon will still take plenty of planning—to make sure that everything goes off without a hitch. Once you've decided on your destination, fill in the honeymoon information below.

Flight Number:	
Departure:	Arrival:
Airport/Station:	
Hotel:	

Check-in:	Check-out:
Car rental:	
Departure:	Arrival:

TO TAKE WITH YOU

- ☐ Traveler's checks
- ☐ Credit cards
- ☐ Driver's and marriage license
- ☐ Passport or visa
- ☐ Address book
- ☐ Guidebook for destination
- ☐ Aspirin
- ☐ Sewing kit

Name Change Checklist

It's still more popular to use your husband's name than to keep your own. So if you are, you'll need to change your name (and your address, if you're moving) on the following papers and documents and for the following agencies:

- ☐ Driver's license
- ☐ Car registration
- ☐ Social Security card
- ☐ Income tax form
- ☐ Voter registration
- ☐ Passport or visa
- ☐ Bank accounts
- ☐ Credit cards
- ☐ Insurance
- ☐ School records
- ☐ Employment records
- ☐ Post office

Part Three:

Our Wedding

Our Photographs

Our Photographs

Our Photographs

Our Stationery and Favors

Attach Sample Here

The Bridal Bouquet

Our Wedding Flowers

Attach Sample/Photo Here

Part Four:
Appendix

SOURCES

UNITED STATES

BAKERIES

ATLANTA

Bread and Pastry Shoppe
535 Indian Trail Rd.
(404) 921-4168

Donuts 'N' Cakes
5615 Memorial Dr.
(404) 292-7609

Glass Oven Bakery
Northlake Mall
(404) 934-2303
Lenox Square
(404) 266-8994
Perimeter Mall
(404) 394-2924

BOSTON

Brookline Bakery
1665 Beacon St.
Brookline, MA
(617) 566-0644

Montilio's
Faneuil Hall
(617) 367-2371

Sweet Presentations
1376 Beacon St.
Brookline, MA
(617) 566-3330

CHICAGO

Bridal Cakes by Rose
4237 West 63rd St.
(312) 735-8677

Davidson's Bakeries
5921 North Broadway
(312) 561-7422
16 East Randolph St.
(312) 332-9070
157 West Madison St.
(312) 322-9335
15 East Washington St.
(312) 332-8507
5921 North Broadway
(312) 561-8055
3201 North Broadway
(312) 549-9393
1663 West Howard St.
(312) 743-9150
1412½ West Morse St.
(312) 743-9120

Ferrara, Incorporated
2210 West Taylor St.
(312) 666-2200

Larry's Bakery, Incorporated
12 Madison Oak Park
(312) 386-2695
(312) 378-1880

Latin American Bakery
1010 West Belmont St.
(312) 477-2320

Moore's Bakery
1235 West 79th St.
(312) 783-6997

Party Cakes Bakery
11820 South Western St.
(312) 233-2450

Phillip's Butter Kist Bakery
1955 West Belmont St.
(312) 281-4150

Roeser's Bakery
3216 West North St.
(312) 489-6900

DALLAS

Aston's English Bakery
6029 Luther Lane
(214) 368-6425

Bake Shoppe
8633 Park Lane
(214) 361-6448

Beach Forest Bakery, Incorporated
5819 Blackwell St.
(214) 368-4490

The French Baker
110 Preston Royal
(214) 369-2253

Lakewood Bakery
2309 Abrams Rd.
(214) 821-4815

Patisserie-Confiserie
6959 Arapaho St.
(214) 386-9886

DENVER

Bell Pastry and Fine Foods Shop
1307 E. Sixth Ave.
(303) 831-7134

Cake Box Bakery
1268 S. Sheridan St.
(303) 935-4248

Child's Bakery Shop
2706 S. Colorado Blvd.
University Hills Shopping Center
(303) 757-1285

Das Meyer Fine Pastry Chalet
9820 W. 44th St.
(303) 425-5616

Dee's Cakes
The Brentwood Center
2037 S. Federal Blvd.
(303) 934-2979

The German Bakery
165 Steele St.
(303) 322-2279

Golden Croissants
3005 South Parker Rd.
Bldg. C, Suite 322
(303) 755-3391

Mayo's Pastry and Pastry Shop
2468 S. Colorado Blvd.
University Hills Shopping Center
(303) 753-6315

Vollmer's Bakery
1500 E. Colfax Ave.
(303) 832-8830

HOUSTON

ABC Bakery Catering & Hallmark
11138 Airline St.
(713) 448-7502

Baker's Pantry, Incorporated
8741 Kay Fwy.
(713) 467-7474

Café de la Paux
863 Frostwood St.
(713) 932-0867

Goldilocks Bake Shop
2401 West Holcombe St.
(713) 665-6464
(713) 665-6527

Hynes Bakery
1719 Houston Ave.
(713) 223-0711

Ladan Pastry Café
11319 Bissonnet St.
(713) 530-2310

Nielsen's Bakery
9625 Bissonnet St.
(713) 771-4833

Olympia Bakery
7653 Clarewood St.
(713) 771-3181

Paris Bakery
8405 Winkler St.
(713) 649-0427

Wedding Cakes by Erma
7103 Langley St.
(713) 633-7200

LOS ANGELES

Daly Bakery & Party Shop
1820 Marengo St.
(213) 222-2656

Kream Krop Bakery
2323 W. Manchester St.
(213) 750-0214

Real Bakery
2922 N. Broadway
(213) 225-8259

Sarno's
1712 Novermont St.
(213) 664-8445
(213) 664-1121

Sorbonne Pastries
1966 Hillhurst St.
(213) 664-0805

NEW ORLEANS

Joe Gambino's
3609 Toledano St.
(504) 822-3340
4821 Veteran's Memorial Blvd.
(504) 885-7500

Lawrence's Bakery
5242 Elysian Fields Ave.
(504) 288-4262

McKenzie's Pastry Shoppes
(General office)
3847 Desire St. Pkwy.
(504) 944-4262

Picou's Bakeries
2501 Bayou Rd.
(504) 974-0412

Swiss Confectionery
606 Frenchmen St.
(504) 943-6653

NEW YORK

The Cake Boutique
1290 Lexington Ave.
(212) 427-3894

Cake Masters
120 West 72nd St.
(212) 787-1414

D'Aiuto's Pastry
405 Eighth Ave.
(212) 564-7136
494 Ninth Ave.
(212) 564-4944
873 Eighth Ave.
(212) 247-1942

DeRobertis Pastry Shop
176 First Ave.
(212) 674-7137

Eclair Pastry
191 West 72nd St.
(212) 873-7700
Grand Central/Lower Level
(212) 684-8877
54th St. and First Ave.
(212) 795-5355

Jon Vie Pastry Shop Incorporated
492 Ave. of the Americas
(212) 242-4440

Maria Quality Pastry Shop, Incorporated
922 Second Ave.
(212) 355-2156

Verniero Pasticceria
342 East 11th St.
(212) 674-7264

SAN FRANCISCO

Adeline of San Francisco
1122 Van Ness St.
(415) 673-5000
17 Kearny St.
(415) 392-9000
1475 Market St.
(415) 864-8000
53 W. Partal St.
(415) 665-1000
22nd and Mission Sts.
(415) 824-3000
2570 Ocean St.
(415) 587-8000
111 Powell St.
(415) 781-3000
986 Mission St.
(415) 546-7000
390 Golden Gate St.
(415) 673-0500

Fantasia
3465 California St.
(415) 752-0825

Hokamp's Bakery
1720 Polk St.
(415) 474-0822

Sugar 'N' Spice
3200 Balboa St.
(415) 387-1722

Victoria Pastry Company
1362 Stockton St.
(415) 781-2015

CATERERS

ATLANTA

A Touch of Taste Incorporated
7528 N. Highland Ave. NE
(404) 875-1184

Bridal Catering
2379 Timber Ridge Ct.
(404) 241-1216

Bridal Center of the South Catering & Flowers Incorporated
2784 Jasmine Ct. NE
(404) 939-2919

Food Management Concepts Incorporated
57 Forsynth St. NW
(404) 586-9825

Julian's Catering
100 Hurst St. NE
(404) 688-5599

BOSTON

Catering to Your Every Whim
341 Beacon St.
Newton, MA
(617) 969-4666

Hillcrest-Nims-Kendall
220 Bear Hill Rd.
Waltham, MA
(617) 890-2644

White Caterers
433 Clinton Rd.
Brookline, MA
(617) 566-4320

CHICAGO

A-Scandinavian American Catering Service
5247 N. Clark St.
(312) 275-6100

Edmunds Catering
5540 N. Milwaukee Ave.
(312) 775-1596

Lonnecke Catering Company
2100 W. Grand St.
(312) 666-6565

Marlene's Catering, Incorporated
5715 S. Kedzie St.
(312) 925-2066

Michael Catering
6128 W. Belmont St.
(312) 736-6232

The Mixing Bowl Limited
1341 N. Sedgewick St.
(312) 664-6900

Peterson Catering & Food Service
3500 N. Cicero Ave.
(312) 725-7455

Prime Food Caterers
5643 W. North St.
(312) 889-3060

DALLAS

A Touch of Gourmet
5000 Belt Line Rd.
(214) 458-1036

Catering Specialties by Vonnal
912 Wateka Wy.
(214) 234-2300

Chimney Restaurant Austrian Swiss Cuisine
973 N. Central Expwy.
(214) 369-6466

Ernie's of Dallas
4412 Lover's Lane
(212) 368-5454

Fairmont Hotel
Ross and Akard Sts.
(214) 368-6151

Flemister's Catering
124 Walnut Hill Village
(213) 350-3610

Reynold's Wedding Service
4906 Leland St.
(214) 421-7248

DENVER

Caterers of Colorado
3653 Navajo St.
(303) 455-1400

The Catering Company
5270 E. Arapahoe Rd.
(303) 773-6324

Chef Leo's Catering
777 Cavosa Ct.
(303) 629-9001

Feast & Company
Third and Detroit Sts.
(303) 399-4440

Gourmet International
3095 Peoria St.
(303) 361-6303

Kenji's Catering, Incorporated
1899 York St.
(303) 399-0547

Singer's Gourmet Catering
303 S. Jasmine St.
(303) 355-4293

HOUSTON

ABC Bakery Catering & Hallmark
11138 Airline St.
(713) 448-7502

Beth's Catering and Floral
1934 Strawberry St.
(713) 472-8029

Carriage Boutique Caterers
7618 Richmond Ave.
(713) 782-5532

Catering by Shirley
4830 Langley St.
(713) 694-3327

Meyerland Club
9000 S. Rice
(713) 666-0201

Mrs. James C. Jenkins Catering Service
1807 Locklaine St.
(713) 472-4994

Towne & Country Caterers
2603 Yost St.
(713) 485-1617

LOS ANGELES

The Casserole
7782 San Fernando Rd.
(213) 875-1958

Damiano Gourmet Catering
1511 S. Robertson St.
(213) 553-4429

Romanoff's
1236 N. Columbus Ave.
(213) 244-2163

NEW ORLEANS

The Carrollton
4710 Carrollton Ave.
(504) 482-1611

Gourmet Food, Incorporated
6504 Spanish Fort Blvd.
(504) 282-4614

Pete Sclafani Restaurant & Caterers
9900 Haynes Blvd.
(504) 241-4472

Royal Orleans Hotel
621 St. Louis St.
(504) 529-5333

NEW YORK

Copacabana
10 E. 60th St.
(212) 755-6010

Dover Caterers
144 E. 57th St.
(212) 759-2570

Garvin's Restaurant
19 Waverly Pl.
(212) 473-5261

New American Catering
210 W. 70th St. #1406
(212) 724-6957

Taylor Maid Service
Lexington Ave.
(212) 767-7171
(212) 838-7171

Townhouse Caterers
215 E. 80th St.
(212) 772-2551

The Warwick
54th St. and Ave. of the Amer.
(212) 247-2700

SAN FRANCISCO

Beacon Street Kitchen
148 Beacon St.
(415) 952-4323
(415) 755-7450

Catering by Upton's
2419 Lombard St.
(415) 567-1335

Knight's Catering & Restaurant
363 Golden Gate Ave.
(415) 861-3312

Max's of San Francisco
1602 Lombard St.
(415) 771-9292

Mi Burrito Taqueria
643 Clay St.
(415) 981-4007

The Town and Country Tea Room
524 Sutter St.
(415) 986-0344

CHINA, CRYSTAL, AND SILVER

ATLANTA

A Proper Setting, Incorporated
4505 Ashford Dunwoody Rd. NE
(404) 396-3700

Glass Etc.
4049 La Vista Rd.
(404) 493-7936

Maier & Berklee
3225 Peachtree Rd.
(404) 261-4911
Perimeter Mall
(404) 396-8011
Cumberland Mall/Upper Level
(404) 432-3167
Southlake Mall/Upper Level
(404) 961-6930

Tiffany & Company
Phipps Plaza
(404) 261-0074

BOSTON

Diane at the Parker House
60 School St.
(617) 426-4932

Frank DePrisco
333 Washington
(617) 227-3339

Jones McDuffy & Stratton
221 N. Beacon St.
(617) 254-0300

Joseph Gann Jewelers
387 Washington St.
(617) 426-4932

Province Jewelry Incorporated
333 Washington St.
(617) 742-1130

Shreve Crump & Lowe
330 Boylston St.
(617) 267-9100

CHICAGO

Borg
6400 N. Harlem St.
(312) 825-2800

The Crystal Cave
1141 N. Michigan Ave.
(312) 787-2147

The Crystal Suite
28 Old Orchard Shopping Center
(312) 677-7180
226 Oakbrook Center Mall
(312) 323-2525
835 N. Michigan Ave.
(312) 944-1320

Princess House Crystal
1608 Hemstock St.
(312) 653-4514

Whitehall China Limited
2024 Northbrook Center
(312) 272-4770

DALLAS

Dabney's
333 Hillside Village
(214) 823-8760

Haltom's Jewelry
5100 Belt Line Rd.
(214) 385-0325

Hutshenreuther Company
2100 N. Stemms Fwy.
(214) 748-1505

The Ivy House
806 Old Town Shopping Center
(214) 369-2411

The Panhandlers
310 Preston Royal Shopping Center
(214) 369-8067

Polly Dupont
360 Promenade South
(214) 235-4715

Serpendipity
1203 Old Town in the Village
(214) 692-0249

The Wedding Registry
5307 E. Mockingbird St.
(214) 824-5391

DENVER

Colorado Culinary, Incorporated
8000 E. Grand Ave.
(303) 696-9034

Courtyard Collection
4940 S. Yosemite St.
(303) 694-6955

Crystal Collection
1265 S. Broadway
(303) 778-1158

Cutco Cutlery & Cookware
7515 W. 17th Ave.
(303) 238-2350

Denver China & Glass
707 Federal Blvd.
(303) 573-0741

Habitat, Incorporated
2080 S. Mavana St.
(303) 755-5311

International Villa
262 Fillmore St.
(303) 333-1524
8101 E. Belleview Dr.
(303) 773-2130

Reeders Hallmark
Aurora Mall
(303) 366-1104
Southwest Plaza
(303) 973-3295

HOUSTON

Bayliwix
4836 Beechnut St.
(713) 665-8454
1981 W. Gray St.
(713) 520-0331
7705 Bellfort St.
(713) 729-4436

Carole Stupell Limited
1800 Post Oak Blvd.
(713) 961-7560

Chinacryst
5501-C FM 1960 W.
(713) 893-7004

Foley's
1110 Main St.
(713) 651-6161

Gazebo Gifts
59 Woodlake Square
(713) 780-1253

Kaplan's Ben Hur
2125 Yale Heights
(713) 861-2121

Spencer's Gallery
11964 Westheimer St.
(713) 497-0106

LOS ANGELES

David Orgell
320 N. Rodeo Dr.
(213) 272-3355

Geary's Beverly Hills
351 N. Beverly Dr.
(213) 272-9334

Ricci
5700 W. Pico Blvd.
(213) 669-0319

Roy Rubens
143 S. Beverly Dr.
(213) 272-1439

Tiffany & Company
9502 Wilshire Blvd.
(213) 273-8880

NEW ORLEANS

Adler's
722 Canal St.
(504) 523-5292

Bruno Galleries
3536 Calhous St.
(504) 866-4511

Dupree's
526 WIlkinson Row
(504) 522-6990

Jay Aronson Limited
Uptown Square
(504) 865-1186

United China and Glass Company
4500 Tchoupitoulas St.
(504) 891-5881

NEW YORK

Cardel Limited
615 Madison Ave.
(212) 753-8880

Ceramic Gift Gallery
1001 Ave. of the Americas
(212) 354-9216

Georg Jenson Silversmiths
683 Madison Ave.
(212) 759-6457

Gimori Fifth Ave.
711 Fifth Ave.
(212) 752-8790

Hempstead China
27 William St.
(212) 344-6970

Michael C. Fina
580 Fifth Ave.
(212) 869-5050

Samuel C. Schecter Silversmiths
29 Park Row
(212) 227-0670

Waterford Crystal
225 Fifth Ave.
(212) 683-8899

SAN FRANCISCO

Fitz & Floyd Fine China
2258A Market St.
(415) 626-7330

Heritage House, Incorporated
2190 Palou Ave.
(415) 285-1331

Paul Bauer, Incorporated
120 Grant Ave.
(415) 421-6862

S. Christian of Copenhagen, Incorporated
225 Post St.
(415) 392-3394

Tiffany & Company
252 Grant Ave.
(415) 781-7000

Wedgewood San Francisco
304 Stockton/Union Square
(415) 391-5610

ENTERTAINMENT

ATLANTA

The Great Southern Sound Company
2533 Peachwood Circle NE
(404) 634-7667

Rising Star Productions
Lawyer's Title Bldg.
(404) 429-8181

Stew Magee Orchestra
508 Park Ave. SE
(404) 624-3300

BOSTON

Jerry Davis Agency
693 Beacon St.
(617) 527-5776

Ruby Newman Orchestras
160 Boylston St.
(617) 527-3210

CHICAGO

Accent on Music
3623 Glenview Rd.
(312) 724-2460

Al Carver Bands
7 W. 1st Hinsdale St.
(312) 323-1329

Music on Wheels
6630 S. Karlon St.
(312) 284-8397

Night Breeze
1245 N. Linden St.
(312) 934-6075

Patti Brian Orchestras & Entertainment
7344 N. Winchester St.
(312) 274-9222

Ralph Sterling Orchestras
2916 W. Estes St.
(312) 764-0209

Stu Hirsch Orchestras
200 Dewey Ave.
(312) 328-4395

DALLAS

Brounoff Orchestra Agency
11851 High Meadow
(214) 247-7430

CR Sheppard Productions
11171 Harry Hines
(214) 243-2997

First Desk Quartet
1733 Oldfield St.
(214) 391-7553

Jerry Samuels
16615 Dundrennan St.
(214) 248-6750

The Sock Hop
2946 W. Northwest Hwy.
(214) 352-6856

DENVER

Action Music Productions
3569 S. Pennsylvania St.
(303) 761-4912

American Consolidated Entertainment Service
7573 E. Costilla Blvd.
(303) 771-4434

Belden's Bands
5600 S. Syracuse Circle
(303) 779-0091

Colorado Sound 'N' Light
703 Plaris Pl.
(303) 429-9111

Jay Wieder Music
1106 Steele St.
(303) 333-0547

Stephen Paul and His Orchestra
9180 W. 90 Pl.
(303) 420-8577

HOUSTON

Aaron & Williams Agency
4615 SW Fwy.
(713) 961-2263

Adams & Green
10555 Northwest Fwy.
(713) 681-5200

Jay M. Burman Orchestra
7634 Clarewood St.
(713) 776-8183

The Jazz Connection
16902 El Camino Real
(713) 488-8350

Music by Ken Turner
7902 Shady Arbor St.
(713) 937-9660

Wedding Music by Tommy Lauer
10300 Mayfield St.
(713) 465-8883

LOS ANGELES

Billy Devroe Orchestras
5000 Los Feliz Blvd.
(213) 666-2666

Disco Party DJ
22223 De La Osa
(213) 347-3954

Keen Clark Combos & Orchestras
5676 Spreading Oak Dr.
(213) 466-6331

Talent World Productions
9601 Wilshire Blvd.
(213) 550-1354

NEW ORLEANS

After Six Entertainment
1365 Perth St.
(504) 246-9320

Musical Contracting Agency
Maison Blanche Bldg.
(504) 542-8359

Omni Attractions
500 Valence St.
(504) 899-8297

Society Jazz Band
628 Dauphine St.
(504) 522-3346

NEW YORK

Jack Adato Music & Entertainment
888 8th Ave.
(212) 582-4600

The Black Tie Strings
72-1537 Ave.
(212) 478-7521

Music A La Mode
11 W. 25th St.
(212) 807-8914

Herbie Rose Entertaining Orchestras
2220 Tiemann Ave.
(212) 882-7750

The Bob Hardwick Sound
770 Lexington Ave.
(212) 838-7521

2001 Entertainers
314 W. 53rd St.
(212) 245-6100

SAN FRANCISCO

Chuck Hamilton Orchestra
1063 Gilman Dr.
(415) 992-3111

Dennis Donovan Music
P.O. Box 15442
(415) 346-2262

FLORISTS

ATLANTA

Flowers by Lucas
100 Peachtree St.
(404) 523-2909

Mary Lee Silks Incorporated
3061-13 Kingston Ct.
(404) 952-2201

Wright's Florist
2393 Peachtree Rd. NE
(404) 233-4446

BOSTON

A Bed of Roses
64 Arlington St.
(617) 451-1148

Berlin Flower Shop
466 Cometh Ave.
(617) 266-6044

Neponset Florist
163 Neponset Ave.
(617) 265-2000

Rob Roy Florists
1892 Centre St.
(617) 323-5900

Village Greenery & Florist Incorporated
618 Washington St.
(617) 254-3523

CHICAGO

Adonna Flower Shops
2959 W. Irving Pk.
(312) 588-6562

Adorn Flower Fashions
4334 W. Lawrence St.
(312) 605 6010

A1-0-Wishes Wedding Flowers
3322 N. Milwaukee Ave.
(312) 736-1555

Belpark Florist
4715 W. Belmont St.
(312) 736-9030

Carriage Flower Shop
2030 W. Mintios St.
(312) 878-4879

Dandy-Lion Florist
5557 W. Belmont St.
(312) 282-1310

Flowers Etcetera by Mana, Incorporated
11105 S. Western St.
(312) 445-1666
3029 E. 91st St.
(312) 734-2222

Flowers Unlimited
8621 S. Stony Island
(312) 978-1333

DALLAS

Arden's Flower Studio
1419 Dragon St.
(214) 747-2207

Arrangements by Bullards
4529 McKinney Ave.
(214) 528-0383

Arrangements by Petals & Stems Florists
13239 Montfort Ave. at LBJ Fwy.
(214) 233-9037

Crest Florist
911 E. Saner St.
(214) 374-8181

Flowers by Cheryl
2729 Motley St.
(214) 279-7709

Forestwood Florist
11818 Inwood Rd.
(214) 233-4762

Ursula's Flower Boutique
902 Hwy. 303
(214) 647-8755

DENVER

Buds 'N' Blossoms Flowers
727 Colorado Blvd.
(303) 388-0802

Floral Elegance Unlimited
2468 S. Colorado Blvd.
(303) 753-1082

Harold's Flowers
6630 E. Colfax Ave.
(303) 388-1666

Interwest Floral Supply
2300 Walton St.
(303) 296-2050

Lady Sue's FLowers
10230 W. 26th Ave.
(303) 232-0733

Loop Flowers Incorporated
1510 California Blvd.
(303) 629-1717
(303) 629-1776

Swiss Flower Shoppe
9840 W. 44th Ave.
(303) 424-7421

Washington Park Florists
1295 S. Vine St.
(303) 778-7146

HOUSTON

A-Daisy-A-Day Florist
1958 FM Rd. 1960 W.
(713) 444-2571

Alice's Florist Flowers Bouquet
4662 Beechnut St.
(713) 664-8813

Allen's Hearts & Flowers
1121 South Ave.
(713) 473-2177

Bouquets by Verdie
939 Pinemont St.
(713) 682-7759

The Boutonniere Florist Incorporated
8726 Stella Link St.
(713) 665-7496

Bridal Flowers by Martinique
2045 Southwest Fwy.
(713) 527-9557

La Mariposa Gardens
1303 Nasa St.
(713) 488-2476

Mary Lou's Florist Boutique Incorporated
11512 Hughes Rd.
(713) 481-6133

LOS ANGELES

Ambassador Florists
3400 Wilshire Blvd.
(213) 384-0421

Carl's Flowers
6081 Sunset Blvd.
(213) 467-5494
(213) 874-6181

Eva's Florist
6007 Hooper Ave.
(213) 231-9801

Fifth Ave. Florist
2924 W. Manchester Blvd.
(213) 758-3111

Fran Pallay Flowers
9201 W. Sunset Blvd.
(213) 272-1794

Los Feliz
1802 N. Hillhurst Ave.
(213) 666-4055

Renee's Flowers
8533 Melrose St.
(213) 655-7532

Venice La Brea Florist
1601 S. La Brea Ave.
(213) 938-3746

NEW ORLEANS

AAA Floral & Wedding Shoppe Incorporated
8601 W. St. Bernard Hwy.
(504) 271-0597

Carrollton Flower Market
838 Dublin St.
(504) 866-9614

Flowers by J & J
1323 Caffin Ave.
(504) 947-0542

The French Quarter Florist
1116 N. Rampart St.
(504) 523-5476

Haydel's Flower Shoppe Incorporated
3730 S. Claiborn Ave.
(504) 891-2848

Rieth the Florist
5080 Pontchartrain Blvd.
(504) 488-3788

NEW YORK

Academy Floral East
1243 Second Ave.
(212) 685-2039
(212) 838-2684

Flora Plenty
1135 First Ave.
(212) 347-4037

Flowers Unlimited
1140 Third Ave.
(212) 535-6255

Golden Fantasy Flower Shop
415 E. 70th St.
(212) 861-1641

June Floral
61 W. 62nd St.
(212) 245-5077

Kyoto Garden Florists
109 E. 42nd St.
(212) 490-8720

New York Flower Market
169 Third Ave.
(212) 228-8510

Plaza Florist, Incorporated
944 Lexington Ave.
(212) 744-0936

Superior Florists
828 Ave. of the Americas
(212) 679-4065

Sutton East Gardens
1159 York Ave.
(212) 838-4585

SAN FRANCISCO

Accent on Flowers
4080 24th St.
(415) 829-3233

Belmont Florist
2360 Fillmore St.
(415) 567-2140

Birmingham's
969 Sutter St.
(415) 775-5566

Gilmour's An Affair with Flowers
2960 16th St.
(415) 431-8787

The Marina Florist
2233 Chestnut St.
(415) 346-6346

Pinelli's Flowerland
714 Clement St.
(415) 751-4142

Sheridan & Bell Florist, Incorporated
120 Maiden La.
(415) 781-2300

Thom & Yvonne's
2277 Chestnut St.
(415) 922-8448

Village Florist
2190 Bush St.
(415) 567-0556

FORMALWEAR

ATLANTA

Atlanta's Tech Shop
623 Spring St. NE
(404) 881-8678
(404) 881-6024

Formal Atlanta
3393 Peachtree Rd. NE
(404) 237-8340

Gingiss Formalwear
Gwinett Place Mall
(404) 476-2100
Cumberland Mall
(404) 436-5292
Northlake Mall
(404) 934-0868
Greenbriar Shopping Center
(404) 349-6590
Southlake Mall
(404) 961-6948
Perimeter Mall
(404) 394-2860

Hills Formal Wear and Tailors
1173-A S. Hairston Rd.
(404) 296-2178

Knight's Formal Wear Incorporated
2089 Monroe Dr. NE
(404) 897-1264

Mitchell's Formal Wear
North Dekalb Mall
(404) 634-6557
3072 Roswell Rd. NW
(404) 261-0022

Ray's
2939 N. Druid Hills Rd. NE
(404) 636-6301

BOSTON

Manhattan Tuxedos of Dedham
283 Washington St.
(617) 326-9888

Mr. Formal Incorporated
1099 Lexington St.
(617) 893-9404

Mr. Saunders Formal Wear
80 Burlington Mall Rd.
(617) 273-3228

Read & White
59 Chaucy St.
(617) 542-7444

Russo's Tux Shop
320 Revere Beach Pkwy.
(617) 889-1004

CHICAGO

Diequez Tuxedo Rental
3335 W. North St.
(312) 392-2110

Gingiss Formalwear
Lake and Dearborn Sts.
(312) 263-7171
The Brickyard
(312) 637-4550
3340 N. Ashland Ave.
(312) 327-5510
Lincoln Village Shopping Center
(312) 267-0300
555 W. 14th Pl.
(312) 829-0001
Ford City Shopping Center
(312) 582-8600

Henry's Formal Wear
5527 S. Harlem St.
(312) 586-9400
3223 W. 63rd St.
(312) 925-0850
4083 Archer Ave.
(312) 523-5924
2216 W. 95th St.
(312) 881-1311

J. Perry Formalwear
Northbrook Ct.
(312) 498-0787

Picardi & Sons
2735 N. Harlem St.
(312) 889-7733

Seno Formal Wear
185 N. State St.
(312) 782-1115
5723 W. Belmont St.
(312) 889-4700
Riverview Plaza Shopping Center
(312) 929-4210

DALLAS

Gentlemen's Quarters
Richardson Square Mall
(214) 231-7188
Prestonwood Town Center
(214) 980-1515

Gingiss Formalwear
2162 Collin Creek Mall
(214) 422-7572
Valley View Mall
(214) 661-0557
Northpark Center
(214) 696-5796

House of Tuxedos
432 Northlake Shopping Center
(214) 349-3600
4009 Northwest Pkwy
(214) 363-8568
Sakowitz Village
(214) 980-0002
1067 Red Bird Mall
(214) 296-2911

Mr. Formal Tuxedo Rentals & Sales
2729 S. Lancaster Rd.
(214) 375-2559
7125 S. Polk St.
(214) 224-5594

Star Formal Wear
9100 N. Central Expwy.
(214) 692-1424
11311 Harry Hines St.
(214) 243-1578

DENVER

A-One Tux Rental
70 Broadway
(303) 722-5046

Fashion Formalwear
8899 N. Washington Blvd.
(303) 289-4722
2968 S. Colorado Blvd.
University Hills Plaza
(303) 753-0321
1892 S. Wadsworth Blvd.
(303) 989-4721

Gingiss Formalwear
8840 W. Colfax Ave.
(303) 238-7748

Randall's
1441 W. 46th Ave.
(303) 455-8064
Northglenn Mall
(303) 452-0608
7400 E. Hampden Ave.
(303) 729-6119

Sir Knight Tuxedos
12 Federal Blvd.
(303) 935-6277

Smiley's Formal Wear Specialists
1028 E. Colfax Ave.
(303) 832-1692

Stan's Tuxedos
7280 Monaco St.
(303) 287-7765

Varsity Formal Wear
70 Broadway
(303) 778-8073

HOUSTON

Al's Formal Wear
121 San Jacinto
(713) 659-4301
18 Braeswood Square
(713) 771-1112

Westheimer 2720 Hillcroft
(713) 781-7191
8452 Gulf Fwy.
(713) 644-3683
Dickinson Plaza Shopping Center
(713) 337-2942
151 Greens Rd.
(713) 443-6420
NW Fwy. 5338 W. 34th St.
(713) 682-1131
19757 Eastex Fwy.
(713) 446-0126
64 E. Crosstimbers St.
(713) 692-6051
606 Memorial City Shopping Center
(713) 464-1693
6563 Fondren Rd.
(713) 778-1630

Mister Penguin Tuxedo Rental & Sales
10830 North Fwy.
(713) 447-0606

Star Formal Wear
9700 Fondren Rd.
(713) 981-0530

Ventura's Formal Wear
102 North Loop West
(713) 880-1661
103 Greenspoint Mall
(713) 448-1384
Cahpions 111 FM 1960
(713) 440-0293
505 Northwest Mall
(713) 688-9487
509 Sharpstown Center
(713) 771-5791
244 Almeda Mall
(713) 941-8446
175 Town & Country Village
(713) 932-1926

LOS ANGELES

Alexander's Discount Tuxedos
624 S. La Brea Ave.
(213) 937-4973

Anthony Loya
5340 Whittier Blvd.
(213) 723-3314

Black Tie Affair
7119 Laurel Canyon Blvd.
(213) 875-0005

Dew Drop Tux Shop
6630 Crenshaw Blvd.
(213) 758-5675

Fegan Tuxedo Rental
3881 S. Western St.
(213) 732-0953
450 W. Adams St.
(212) 731-8189

Lovell's Formal Wear
3925 S. Vermont St.
(213) 735-1271

Ryder's Tuxedo Shop
5108 Wilshire Blvd.
(213) 933-5537

Tuxedo Center
5317 Melrose Ave.
(213) 466-5324

NEW ORLEANS

Gemelle's
117 Camp St.
(504) 522-5223
Cateau Village Shopping Center
(504) 468-2973

Gingiss Formalwear
212 Uptown Square
(504) 861-3676

Holmes Formal Wear Rental
811 Canal St.
(504) 561-6460

Maison Blanche
Clearview Shopping Center
(504) 888-7200
Plaza Lake Forest
(504) 241-8121
Westside Shopping Center
(504) 362-5300

NEW YORK

After Six Incorporated
1674 Broadway
(212) 664-8066

A.T. Harris
47 E. 44th St.
(212) 682-6325

Baldwin Formals
52 W. 56th St.
(212) 245-8190

Dante Lordae Tuxedos
2418 Broadway
(212) 799-9160
1537 Second Ave.
(212) 535-8352
451 Columbus Ave.
(212) 799-9180
858 Second Ave.
(212) 661-0181

Herman's Formal Wear
1190 Ave. of the Americas
(212) 245-2277

Jack & Company
128 E. 86th St.
(212) 722-4455

Lawson Formal Wear
93 Nassau St.
(212) 962-2517

S & L
145 W. 42nd St.
(212) 582-3858

Zeller Tuxedos
201 E. 56th St.
(212) 355-0707

SAN FRANCISCO

Black & White Formal Attire
1211 Sutter St.
(415) 673-0626

Grodin's
Stockton at Market Sts.
(415) 391-8300
Three Embarcadero
(415) 397-8700
Stonestown Mall
(415) 661-7111

Selix
123 Kearney St.
(415) 382-1133
2622 Ocean Ave.
(415) 333-2412

Tuxedo King
2093 Mission St.
(415) 552-7613

Tuxedo Shop
One Embarcadero Center/Podium Level
(415) 433-5353
140 Geary St./Union Square
(415) 391-5325

GOWNS

ATLANTA

Ann Barge for Brides Limited
3210 Paces Ferry Pl. NW
(404) 237-0898

Belle's & Beau's Bridal and Formal Wear
720 N. Glynn St.
(404) 461-4818

Bridals by Lori
6038 Sandy Springs Circle NE
(404) 252-8767

Bride Beautiful
4400 Ashford Dunwoody Rd. NE
(404) 394-2177

Decatur Gown & Bridal
117 E. Court Square
(404) 373-4696

BOSTON

Alyce's Bridals of Chestnut Hill
612 Hammond St.
(617) 277-6550

Brides's World Limited
220 Parsons St.
(617) 782-4454

Emma's of Dedham
Dedham Square
(617) 326-5511

Mary Burns Bridal Shop
87 Summer St.
(617) 338-8033

Pronuptia Bridals, Incorporated
38 Newton St.
(617) 536-0666

Rose Cherubini
234 Clarendon St.
(617) 424-1210

CHICAGO

Bridal Showroom
300 W. Grand St.
(312) 664-6770

Dora La Coutre
8246 S. Kimbark St.
(312) 374-8863

Eva's Bridal & Fashions
5705 W. Belmont St.
(312) 637-7900
7730 N. Elmwood Pkwy.
(312) 452-7711
4811 W. 95 Oak Lawn
(312) 422-5599

Grace Bridal
3209 N. Central St.
(312) 282-0566

Kristina's Bridals & Formals
2842 W. 63rd St.
(312) 471-1559

Laura Lee Bridal Salon
2818 N. Milwaukee Ave.
(312) 384-9807

Margie Bridals
4848 W. Irving Park
(312) 286-5990

Something New Bridal
2714 W. Touhy St.
(312) 274-3357

DALLAS

The Bridal Circle
15101 Midway Rd.
(214) 386-6289

Francine
4009 Northwest Pkwy.
(214) 363-7893
432 Northlake Shopping Center
(214) 349-3600
1067 Red Bird Mall
(214) 296-2911
Sakowitz Village
(214) 480-0002

La Novia Elegante
189 Pleasant Grove Shopping Center
(214) 398-9513

Mockingbird Bridal Boutique
5602 E. Mockingbird La.
(214) 823-6873

Myrel's Bridal Salon
1811 N. Belt Line Rd.
(214) 790-8408

Rone of Dallas
1826 Abrams St.
(214) 823-1793

Shirley's Wedding World
1930 E. Abrams St.
(214) 469-1113

DENVER

A Bride's Boutique
2712 S. Havana St.
(303) 337-3128

Bridals by Ferndales
3424 S. Broadway
(303) 761-2064

Colorado's Bridal Center
3924 S. Broadway
(303) 761-2064

Lehrer's Bridal Village
2100 W. Mississippi Ave.
(303) 937-7600

Mayo's Wedding World
2968 S. Colorado Blvd.
(303) 753-0347

Pearl-Scott Classics Custom Bridal Gowns
3205 W. 26th Ave.
(303) 455-8899

Schaffer's Bridal Shop
1525 Stout St.
(303) 893-5885

Wedding Showcase
Federal Blvd.
(303) 935-2444

HOUSTON

Bridal Elegance
14013 Memorial St.
(713) 493-6070

Bridal Fashions
2129 FM 1960 W.
(713) 893-9991

Bride 'N' Formal
7811 Mount at Kiry Sts.
(713) 791-1886
1208 San Jacinto at Polk Sts.
(713) 652-0861
149 Greens Rd.
(713) 821-1611
8452 Gulf Fwy. Monroe East
(713) 644-8295
609 Memorial City Shopping Center
(713) 465-5429
64 E. Crosstimbers St.
(713) 692-9105

Brides by Shirley
2200 Main St.
(713) 659-8787

Modern Bridal & Boutique
5411 FM 1960 W.
(713) 444-2697

Renee's Bridal Fashions
6326 Gulf Fwy.
(713) 644-9752

Ventura's Bridal Fashions
102 N. Loop West
(713) 880-2364

LOS ANGELES

Amalia Originals
365 N. Camden Dr.
(213) 276-4896

The Bridal Party by Kay Joyce
8401 Wilshire Blvd.
(213) 653-3331

Lucille's Bridal and Formal Shop
405 S. Fairfax Ave.
(213) 655-3372

Morrera Studio
140 S. Beverly Dr.
(213) 271-8328

Sussy's Brides & Formals
307 W. 6th St.
(213) 626-9010

Vicky's Bride & Groom
2401 N. Broadway
(213) 228-9370

Wilshire Bridal Salon
3818-22 Wilshire Blvd.
(213) 388-2297

NEW ORLEANS

The Fleur de Lis
4707 Downman Rd.
(504) 242-3711

House of Broel
2220 St. Charles Ave.
(504) 522-2220

Modern Bridal Limited
Westside Shopping Center
(504) 367-4630

Winderella's Bridal Salon, Incorporated
2325½ Metairie Rd.
(504) 833-5574

NEW YORK

Ada Athanassiou
525 Seventh Ave.
(212) 944-8130

Alfred Angelo Inc.
1385 Broadway
(212) 354-6315

Arden's
1014 Sixth Ave.
(212) 391-6968

Bridal Couture
1385 Broadway
(212) 921-4244

Brideland
255 W. 34th St.
(212) 244-8916

Diamond Bridal Collection
1385 Broadway
(212) 302-0212

Georgette
780 Madison Ave.
(212) 517-8176

La Casa de las Novias
170 E. 116th St.
(212) 722-3348

Lo: New York
22 Greenwich Ave.
(212) 741-9285

Lovece Limited
499 Seventh Ave.
(212) 564-7560

Mendicino
1385 Broadway
(212) 221-0085

SAN FRANCISCO

Beaux and Belles Bridal Boutique
1933 Union St.
(415) 922-3035

Dana's Fashions
2748 Wesson St.
(415) 282-7862

Lorrie Deb/Emma Domb
5700 Third St.
(415) 822-6600

Tina's Bridal Shop
2217 California St.
(415) 922-9685

JEWELERS

ATLANTA

Cumberland Diamond Exchange
2756 Hargrove Rd.
(404) 434-4367

The Gold Works
978 N. Main St.
(404) 469-8325

Lauderhills Fine Jewelry
2090 Dunwoody Club Dr.
(404) 396-0462

Pickens, Incorporated
446-A E. Paces Ferry Rd. NE
(404) 237-7885

Universal Diamonds Corporation
3390 Peachtree Rd. NE
(404) 237-1050

Walter R. Thomas Jewelers
2955-A N. Druid Hills Rd. NE
(404) 634-3197
2971 Cobb Pkwy. NE
(404) 955-0736

BOSTON

Coronet Jewelry Company
333 Washington St.
(617) 227-1969

47th St. Jewelry Store
36 Province St.
(617) 423-4124

Jewelers Guild
44 Bromfield St.
(617) 227-4092

John Agliro
333 Washington St.
(617) 367-2468

Marquis Jewelers
Rt. 9
(617) 964-0610

Siedlers
333 Washington St.
(617) 227-5790

Stowell's Jewelers
24 Winter St.
(617) 542-5670

CHICAGO

A. Esses & Son, Incorporated
630 W. Jackson Blvd.
(312) 332-8616

Al Arof
5 S. Wabash St.
(312) 726-1490

Arencibia Jewelry
2710 N. Milwaukee Ave.
(312) 342-7070

Carter Jewelers
Madison and State Sts.
(312) 236-3000

Jan Dee Jewelry
2308 N. Central St.
(312) 871-2222

JB Robinson Jewelers
Brickyard Mall
(312) 745-7700
Chicago Ridge Mall
(312) 425-7550

Purelku Jewelers
2001 W. Irving Park Rd.
(312) 525-1011

Reichman Jewelers
4940 S. Ashland St.
(312) 332-1466

DALLAS

Ben Morris Jewelry Company
4417 Lovers La.
(214) 526-7565

Buckle & Abeita Jewelers
12215 Court St.
(214) 661-2879

Herbert Goldberg Wholesale Jewelers
Pratern Bldg.
(214) 748-8282

Jerry Utay Incorporated
5580 LBJ Fwy.
(214) 386-7482

Lloyd's Credit Jewelers
207 W. Jefferson Blvd.
(214) 941-4084

Wedding Rings Limited
5425 Belt Line Rd.
(214) 934-1105

DENVER

Cory Jewelers
404 16th St.
(303) 825-4227

Eugene Rose
740 S. Colorado Blvd.
(303) 759-3900

Golden Creations Limited
Southglenn Mall
(303) 797-8444

Hess Jewelry
8550 W. Colfax Ave.
(303) 233-3909

JC Keepsake Diamond Center
Aurora Mall
(303) 344-4744
Northglenn Mall
(303) 450-9374
Southwest Plaza
(303) 979-9281
Westminister Mall
(303) 427-9497

Molberg's
2700 S. Colorado Blvd.
(303) 757-8325

HOUSTON

Camilio's Jewelry Company
9355 Long Pt.
(713) 464-2432

Champions Village III
5403-A FM Rd. 1960 W.
(713) 537-6641
12823 Gulf Fwy.
(713) 484-4435

Heller Gem Company
1900 W. Loop South
(713) 961-3864

JC Sloan Company
810 Milan St.
(713) 654 0990
6100 Westheimer
(713) 760-3555

Levit's
2031 S Post Oak Rd.
(713) 622-4950

Michael's
Galleria II/Upper Level
(713) 961-9038
8020 S. Gressner St.
(713) 776-3182
N. Braeswood at Chimney Rock Sts.
(713) 721-4914
FM 1960 at Stuebner Airline
(713) 893-2430

Paul's Jewelry
Northline Mall
(713) 692-6015

Rings by Morrow
Galleria
(713) 627-2285

LOS ANGELES

Coronet Jewelers
138 W. 7th St.
(213) 622-9387

Dadanian Brothers
607 South Hill
(213) 627-1595

David's Jewelers
505 S. Flower
(213) 628-0141

Navarro's Creations
9010 Wilshire Blvd.
(213) 271-2584

The Polomar Company
1515 S. Main St.
(213) 746-0745

Shaw Diamond Company
220 W. Fifth St.
(213) 626-3111

NEW ORLEANS

Canal Jewelry Company
914 Canal St.
(504) 525-9392

Carmouch Jewelers
4524 Shores Dr.
(504) 885-7549

Fischer's Jewelry
1205 Rampart St.
(504) 524-3355

P.E.M.`Jewelers Incorporated
6601 Veterans Memorial Blvd.
(504) 455-1191

Salloum's Jewelry Company
222 Carondelet St.
(504) 581-5678

Thomas Custon Design Jewelry
Uptown Square
(504) 861-7566

NEW YORK

American Wemp Corporation
695 Fifth Ave.
(212) 751-4884

Cresco Jewelry, Incorporated
657 W. 181st St.
(212) 923 6063

Fortunoff's
681 Fifth Ave.
(212) 758-6660

Gastrich Jewelers
215 E. 86th St.
(212) 289-7558

Gold Post Jewelers Limited
100 WIlliam St.
(212) 344-8540

Mikal Diamonds, Inc.
10 W. 47th St.
(212) 869-0229

Mitchell's Place, Incorporated
18 Park Ave.
(212) 267-8156

NBK Company
215 Park Ave. S.
(212) 982-7700

Wedding Ring Originals
691 Lexington Ave.
(212) 751-3940

Wedding Rings, Incorporated
50 W. 8th St.
(212) 533-211N

SAN FRANCISCO

Azevedo
210 Post St.
(415) 781-0063

Boitano's Jewelry
388 22nd Ave.
(415) 221 4580

Cresalia Jewelers
278 Post St.
(415) 781-7371

Polinski & Son
76C Market St.
(415) 781-6541

Theodora
50 Post St.
(415) 398-7464

PHOTOGRAPHERS

ATLANTA

Andrew Watson Photography
3306 Sims Rd.
(404) 979-0150

Barbaro Studios
1006 Huntington Ct. St.
(404) 296 5624

David Underwood's Studio of Photography
110 Avondale Rd.
(404) 292-6119

Foster & Associates
1012 Piedmont Ave. NE
(404) 892-3533

Phainein Photography
2970 Peachtree Rd. NW
(404) 237-7476

BOSTON

Bachrach Photographers
647 Boylston St.
(617) 536-4730

Bestway Graphic Company
14 Main St.
(617) 623-1517

Lockwood Weddings
580 High St.
(617) 329-5159

Pagar Studio
378 Granite Ave.
(617) 696-7560

Paul Black
1 Craigie St.
(617) 492-5369

Sharon's Studio
171 Neponset Ave.
(617) 288-5511

Starling Photography Studio
663 Warren St.
(617) 427 4400

CHICAGO

Al's Candid Photos
2719 W. 43rd St.
(312) 927-6288

Black Image Productions
843 E. 79th St.
(312) 487-9374

Color Photo Studio
1811 W. 35th St.
(312) 847-7300

Curtiss Bridal Services
837 S. Westmore Ave.
(312) 923-4242

D'Lara Photography
3344 W. 111th St.
(312) 239-7369

Edward Fox Photography
4900 N. Milwaukee Ave.
(312) 736-0200

Jan's Photo Services
5712 S. Pulaski St.
(312) 735-4122

Professional Wedding Photographers
3930 N. Pine Grove St.
(312) 248-1255

Rembrandt Studios
4401 S. Harlem St.
(312) 788-5600
3121 N. Central St.
(312) 545-1550
13020 S. Western St.
(312) 388-8848
4748 S. Pulaski St.
(312) 376-0600
3710 W. 26th St.
(312) 522-3388
4909 S. Ashland St.
(312) 254-7554

DALLAS

A Brides Dream by Gary Studios
2358 Oates Dr.
(214) 327-7383

A-1 Wedding Photography
912 Via Avenida
(214) 270-1877

Bob Bogen Photography
808 Edgefield Dr.
(214) 235-0101

Dean Eisen Wedding Photography
2121 Trelles Pl.
(214) 231-9090

Geddies of Dallas Photography
5409 N. Jim Miller St.
(214) 381-2129

Hodges Photographers
435 Lovers La.
(214) 526-7451

Puckett Wedding & Photography
336 W. Davis St.
(214) 946-7277

Stringfellow
425 N. Central Expy.
(214) 690-3134

DENVER

Camera 5 Photography
3333 S. Tamarac Dr.
(303) 695 1588

Conover Photography & Weddings
2925 E. Maplewood Ave.
(303) 797-3888

Everett Bennet
1422 E. Fourth Ave.
(303) 366-4959

Ken Stevenson Wedding Photography
3373 S. Niagra Wy.
(303) 758-6308

Rue Len Wedding Photography
488 Thor Ct.
(303) 770-4796

Specialized Wedding Photography
7413 W. Grandview Ave.
(303) 425-6077

HOUSTON

Braden Studio of Photography
1207 S. Sheperd St.
(713) 523-7331

Bridal Photography by Todd Riggle
1009 Patricia Dr.
(713) 479-6459

Broadway Photography
3526 E. Broadway Pearland
(713) 485-1188

Carter Prestige Portraiture
9804 Hillcroft St.
(713) 723-0785

M & M Video Systems, Incorporated
4401 S. Main St.
(713) 523-6369

Roy Arnold Photography
11247 Newton St.
(713) 946-1778

William & Mary Photography
1511 Welch St.
(713) 522-4391

LOS ANGELES

Alfred & Fabris Studios
3012 Wilshire Blvd.
(213) 387-2251

Charles Studios
6513 Hollywood Blvd.
(213) 467-2420

Leroy Brooks Photography
2139 W. Manchester Ave.
(213) 759-6041

Sunshine Photographers
316 S. La Brea Ave.
(213) 931-1139

Vaness & Manchester
2139 W. Manchester St.
(213) 759-6041

Wilson Streamline Photos
5850 S. Vermont Ave.
(213) 750-3838

NEW ORLEANS

Allyn Photography Studios
316 William David Pkwy.
(504) 834-2633

Creative Images
2617 David Dr.
(504) 888-5990

Curtis Liverett
7190 Downman Rd.
(504) 241-3587

Paul Daigvepont Studio
3848 Veterans Memorial Blvd.
(504) 888-4201

Paul W. Malone Photographer
1211 St. Charles Ave.
(504) 524-9253

Photoworks
1822 Robert St.
(504) 891-7747

Potier's Photography
3308 Cleary Ave.
(504) 455-7784

NEW YORK

Antone Photographers
1018 Lexington Ave.
(212) 535-5575

Chelsea Photographers
126 W. 22nd St.
(212) 206-1499

The Photography Bureau, Incorporated
525 West End Ave.
(212) 799-4868

Portraits by Giovan
1290 Madison Ave.
(212) 289-7001

Tara Studios
34 E. 23rd St.
(212) 260-8280

Thornton Studio, Incorporated
18 W. 27th St.
(212) 685-1725

Videoccasions
38 W. 94th St.
(212) 666-5900

Yorkville Photo Studio
166 E. 86th St.
(212) 289-1449

SAN FRANCISCO

Customari Photography
3992 25th St.
(415) 821-4643

DJ Photography Studios
3334 Sacramento St.
(415) 346-5237

Dore Studio
2442 Mission St.
(415) 282-3324

Frank Castro & Maureen Foster Photography
144 W. Protal Ave.
(415) 681-1817

Gabriel Moulin Studio
465 Green St.
(415) 362-6680

Master Wedding Photographers
4721 Geary Blvd.
(415) 221-2295

Miller-Saul Wedding Photography
145 Maywood Dr.
(415) 584-1333

Rey Guila Photography
595 Mission St.
(415) 543-7440

STATIONERS

ATLANTA

A to Z Wedding Supplies Impressions Unlimited
2715 Veltre Pl SW
(404) 696-7836

Alco Printing
1739 Tully Cr. NE
(404) 636-5696

Anthony's Printing Incorporated
335 Peachtree St. NE
(404) 524-6924

Arrow Press Incorporated
685 N. Central Ave.
(404) 761-2474

Associated Paper & Supply Company
3406 Clairmont St.
(404) 636-5781

Bill's
3756 Roswell Rd. NE
(404) 237-5186

Connie's Hallmark
Northlake Mall
(404) 934-1163

Edwards Printing Incorporated
676 Angler Ave. NE
(404) 221-0461

BOSTON

Broadway Stationers
31 Central Square East
(617) 569-1548

Finch Engraving Company
368 Congress Ave.
(617) 542-6857

Maran Printing Service Incorporated
1406 Massachusetts Ave.
(617) 648-9403

The Office Shop of Copley Square
545 Boyleston St.
(617) 437-1090

Russo's Wedding Service
312 Highland Ave.
(617) 666-0320

Twentieth Century Press
266 Summer St.
(617) 423-2616

CHICAGO

Arden Party Printers, Incorporated
4019 W. Irving Park Rd.
(312) 777-5500

Beaux Arts Publishing Company
1234 E. 47th St.
(312) 624-7822

Bride's Dream Chest
3237 W. 63rd St.
(312) 778-5557

Carla's Hallmark
3348 W. Belmont St.
(312) 478-4355

Jan Weber, Incorporated
912 N. Michigan Ave.
(312) 280-0527

Poke-A-Bout Shoppe
854 W. Belmont St.
(312) 477-7466

United Novelty Manufacturing Company
3827 W. Fullerton St.
(312) 278-6211

DALLAS

A Write Occasion
4930 Belt Line Rd.
(214) 458-7997

Card Nook & Gift Shop
6403 Hillcrest Ave.
(214) 528-8955

CK Graphics
11078 Morrison St.
(214) 247-1427

Cliff's Printing
Capital Bank Bldg.
(214) 361-9256
5307 E. Mockingbird La.
(214) 527-6130
Merchants State Bank Bldg.
(214) 826-8911
2 Hillcrest Green Bldg.
(214) 980-4716
Glen Lakes Tower
(214) 696-6625
609 W. Centerville Rd.
(214) 840-8782
Lakewood Bank Tower
(214) 824-8110

Fabsco Gifts & Monograms
6434 E. Mockingbird La.
(214) 826-0620

Paper Place
183 The Quadrangle
(214) 748-2426

Supreme Engraving Company Incorporated
3205 Oak Grove
(214) 521-3608

DENVER

Cherry Creek Card & Party Shop
Cherry Creek Shopping Center
(303) 377-7477

Creative Arts Printing
1452 S. Colorado Blvd.
(303) 753-1563

Crown House Cards & Gifts
North Valley Shopping Center
(303) 287-2482
Aurora Mall Shopping Center
(303) 341-0685

Merritt Paper Company
7565 S. University Blvd.
(303) 797-0206
8490 W. Colfax Ave.
(303) 233-3940

Mr. Business Card
970 Lincoln St.
(303) 832-4047

Paper Wares
2223 W. 50th Ave.
(303) 691-0723

William Ernest Brown
8101 E. Belleview Ave.
(303) 771-2774

HOUSTON

Bartley House
44 Town & Country Village
(713) 821-0100

The Bee Tree
10136 Hammerly
(713) 464-3840

Gene Swinney's Hallmark
702 Memorial City Mall
(713) 461-2700

Salagar Printing Company
7814 Ave. H
(713) 926-6547

Sandy's Hallmark Gifts
11200 Fondren Rd.
(713) 981-1717
10855 Westheimer St.
(713) 975-8941

The Sevretariat Wedding Service
12966 Westhill St.
(713) 497-0976

Witts Gift & Party House
1032 S. Tatar St.
(713) 473-4437

Yours Truly Stationery & Invitations
2431 Rice Blvd.
(713) 529-4836
5482-A FM 1960 W.
(713) 893-2517

LOS ANGELES

Aadco Rents
809 S. La Brea Ave.
(213) 938-7168

Gregory Printing Company
9364 Culver Blvd.
(213) 870-4539

Jordan Matthews
275 S. Robertson Blvd.
(213) 657-0296

Kay Stationers
1833 W. 8th St.
(213) 483-7297

Manchester Invites
2115 W. Manchester St.
(213) 752-8210

Paper House
6107 W. 3rd St.
(213) 937-5710

NEW ORLEANS

Gem Printing Company
1904 Veterans Memorial Blvd.
(504) 831-1762

The Party Basket Limited
739 Nashville Ave.
(504) 891-0093

Seiffert & Sons, Incorporated
609 Baronne St.
(504) 529-4621
351 Airline Hwy.
(504) 833-3728

NEW YORK

Amal Printing & Publishing Corporation
630 Fifth Ave.
(212) 247-3270

B. Proctor Press
150 Fulton St.
(212) 267-0588

Flair Printing Corporation
8 W. 45th St.
(212) 575-0088

Kroll Stationers
145 E. 54th St.
(212) 541-5000

Prowler & Samuels
55 Vandam St.
(212) 924-7232

Ropal Incorporated
1283 Third Ave.
(212) 988-3548

Royal Letter Company, Incorporated
122 E. 42nd St.
(212) 697-2595

SAN FRANCISCO

The Bell Bazaar
3030 16th St.
(415) 861-2824

The Desk Set
3252 Sacramento St.
(415) 921-9575

Jacki Paper
94 Jackson St.
(415) 956-0252
1 Embarcadero Center
(415) 986-6009

Paper World
50 Maiden La.
(415) 421-0209
Crocker Galeria
(415) 391-1700

CANADA

BAKERIES

BRITISH COLUMBIA

BON TON
874 Granville
Vancouver

CHEZ-MOI FANTASY CAKES
11178-84th Ave.
North Delta

THE VALLEY BAKERY
4058 E. Hastings
Vancouver

ONTARIO

JOHN BAIRD SCOTTISH BAKERY
4 Eglinton Sq.
Scarborough

DELIS BAKERY & PASTRY
800 Hunt Club Rd.
Ottawa

M. GRANOWSKA SPECIALISTS
175 Roncevalles
Toronto

HOUSE OF CAKES
7370 Woodbine Ave.
Toronto

McCALL'S QUALITY CAKES
3864 Bloor St. W.
Toronto

NEW ATHENS BAKERY
2811 Eglinton Ave. E.
Scarborough

RIDEAU BAKERY
384 Rideau Dr.
Ottawa

CATERERS

BRITISH COLUMBIA

A Touch of Class Catering, Limited
Victoria

Gala Quality Catering, Limited
Victoria

ONTARIO

Bersani & Carlevale
Toronto

Daniel & Daniel
Toronto

Dinah's Cupboard
Toronto

Gemelli Caterers
Ottawa

Maxine Chetwynd Deli & Fine Foods
Ottawa

Menus Gastronomiques
Toronto

Walter Coles' Sons, Limited
Toronto

QUEBEC

By George!
Montreal

Ritz Catering Service
Ritz-Carlton Hotel
Montreal

Roger Colas Traiteur
Montreal

CHINA, CRYSTAL, AND SILVER

ALBERTA

Dansk
Southgate Centre
111th & 51st Ave.
Edmonton
Denada Gifts Ltd.
3915-51 St. SW
Calgary

ONTARIO

William Ashley
50 Bloor St. W.
Toronto

Bronson's China & Gifts
72 Steeles Ave. W.
Thornhill

De Witt Jewellers
5 Vyner Rd.
Toronto

The Gallery
182-1/2 Charlotte St.
Peterborough

Goodman's China & Gifts
221 Wilmington Ave.
Downsview

Grant's China & Gifts
970 Eglinton Ave. W.
Toronto

Jolanta Interiors
2368 Bloor St. W.
Toronto

QUEBEC

Caplan-Duval
Plaza Cote-des-Neiges
Montreal

ENTERTAINMENT

BRITISH COLUMBIA

Music Makers Dance Music Service
175-800 McBride
New Westminster

Garry Robertson Music Services
101A-2849 North Rd.
Burnaby

ONTARIO

555 Disc Jockeys, Inc.
Northtown Shopping Centre
5385 Yonge St.
Willowdale

Rousseau/Carlton Flute & Guitar Duo
9 Adelpha Dr.
Toronto

QUEBEC

Action Audio
7070 Terrebonne
Montreal

FLORISTS

BRITISH COLUMBIA

Island Florist
Victoria

Old Fashioned Flowers
Victoria

Victoria Fine Flowers
Victoria

ONTARIO

Blossoms
Toronto

Ellis Flowers
Toronto

Eunice Denby, Limited
Toronto

Forest Hill Florists
Ottawa

Susan Belyea Designs
Toronto

Tidy's
Toronto

Van Nes Flowers
Toronto

QUEBEC

Atelier de Montreal
Montreal

Bernard Perreault
Montreal

Fer-Ni Fleurs
Montreal

Lesperance Madame
Montreal

GOWNS

BRITISH COLUMBIA

Bridal Lane
Victoria

Lady Eve Bridal
Vancouver

Parkside Bridal Boutique
Victoria

ONTARIO

The Bridal Loft
Alan Cherry
Toronto

The Creeds Bride
Creeds
Toronto

Jean Pierce Fashions
Toronto

Ritche Bridal Salon
Toronto

Tiffany's Fashions
Ottawa

QUEBEC

Julia of Snowdon
Montreal

La Jeunesse
Montreal

Lia Creations
Montreal

Pronuptia de Paris
Montreal

Sposabella
Montreal

JEWELERS

BRITISH COLUMBIA

George Adam Goldsmith, Ltd.
470 Granville
Vancouver

Brinkhaus Jewellers, Ltd.
701 W. Georgia
Vancouver

Tony Cavelti, Ltd.
692 Seymour
Vancouver

Facet Jewellery Design Studio
Suite 1-2140 41st Ave.
Kerrisdale
Vancouver

Hyart Gems, Ltd.
1055 W. Georgia
Vancouver

ONTARIO

Cartier-Creeds
45 Bloor St. W.
Toronto

DeWitt Jewellers
5 Vyner Rd.
Toronto

European Jewellery
111 Bloor St. W.
Toronto

Interesting Jewellery
685 Yonge St.
Toronto

Secrett Jewel Salon
14 Ave. Rd.
Toronto

QUEBEC

Gerard & Fils Bijtrs. (Anjou), Inc.
7593 les Galeries d'Anjou
Montreal

Lapidarius Joaillier Orfevre
Place Bonaventure
Montreal

Turcot Joaillers
1050 de la Gauchetiere
Montreal

PHOTOGRAPHERS

BRITISH COLUMBIA

The Old Master's Portrait Studio
Victoria

Soft-Light Studio
Victoria

ONTARIO

Bill Browne Studios
Toronto

Jean des Roches Bridal Photographers
Ottawa

Coronet Wedding Photographers
Ottawa

Couvrette
Ottawa

Rod Crookston
Toronto

QUEBEC

Hoffer Portrait Studio
Montreal

Les Studios de Photographie Unis
Montreal

Studio Marc Beaudoin
Laval

REGISTRIES

The Bay
stores throughout Canada

Eaton's
stores throughout Canada

Simpsons
stores throughout Canada

ONTARIO

Henry Birks & Son
Toronto

Holt Renfrew
Toronto

McIntosh & Watts, Limited
Ottawa

William Ashley
The Holt Renfrew Centre
Toronto

STATIONERY

BRITISH COLUMBIA

Alert Stationers, Ltd.
2535 E. Hastings
Burnaby

Bride's Room
244 W. Broadway
Vancouver

Buchan's Kerrisdale Stationeries, Ltd.
4178 Main St.
Vancouver

RSVP
140 Oakridge
Vancouver

ONTARIO

Paper People
218 Yonge St.
Toronto

QUEBEC

Un Peu de Tout Inc.
4965 Queen Mary
Montreal

Plume-au-Vent, Inc.
4436 Wellington
Montreal

INDEX

I

J

L

M

N

O

P

R

S

T

U

V

W